T0023448

Birds *of* Nevada

Field Guide

Stan Tekiela

PUBLICATIONS
Adventure
an imprint of AdventureKEEN

Edited by Sandy Livoti, Jenna Barron, and Brett Ortler

Cover, book design and illustrations by Jonathan Norberg

Range maps produced by Anthony Hertzel

Cover photo: Steller's Jay by Stan Tekiela
All photos by Stan Tekiela except p. 218 (female) by **aaltair/Shutterstock**; p. 340 (male) by **Agami Photo Agency/Shutterstock.com**; p. 334 (non-breeding male) by **Paul Bannick**; p. 224 (juvenile) by **Albert Barr/Shutterstock.com**; p. 124 (main) by **Gareth Bogdanoff/Shutterstock.com**; pp. 72 (female), 104 (female), 134 (both), 206 (all), 294 (main), 302 (both), 304 (both), 334 (female), 336 (both) by **Rick & Nora Bowers**; p. 252 (displaying) by **cliff collings/Shutterstock.com**; pp. 158 (displaying), 266 (displaying) by **Dudley Edmondson**; p. 44 (main) by **A. G. Nelson/Dembinsky Photo Associates**; p. 236 (main) by **Scenic Corner/Shutterstock.com**; pp. 102 (gray-headed), 230 (gray-headed), 340 (female) by **Brian E. Small**; p. 78 (female) by **Sundry Photography/Shutterstock.com**; p. 118 (female) by **vagabond54/Shutterstock.com**; pp. 234 (female), 308 (female) by **vagabond54/Shutterstock.com**; pp. 42 (juvenile), 144 (juvenile & in-flight juvenile), 196 (dark morph, intermediate morph & soaring dark morph), 200 (juvenile), 212 (juvenile), 270 (juvenile), 272 (in-flight juvenile) by **Brian K. Wheeler**; pp. 118 (male), 308 (male) by **wildphoto3/Shutterstock.com**; and pp. 84 (main), 102 (Oregon female), 192 (female), 246 (brown morph), 268 (main), 274 (female), 326 (female) by **Jim Zipp**.

To the best of the publisher's knowledge, all photos were of live birds. Some were photographed in a controlled condition.

10 9 8 7 6 5 4 3 2 1

Birds of Nevada Field Guide
First Edition
Copyright © 2024 by Stan Tekiela
Published by Adventure Publications
An imprint of AdventureKEEN
310 Garfield Street South
Cambridge, Minnesota 55008
(800) 678-7006
www.adventurepublications.net
LCCN 2023028515 (print); 2023028516 (ebook)
ISBN 978-1-64755-421-7 (pbk.); ISBN 978-1-64755-422-4 (ebook)

TABLE OF CONTENTS

WHY WATCH BIRDS IN NEVADA?

Millions of people have discovered bird feeding. It's a simple and enjoyable way to bring the beauty of birds closer to your home. Watching birds at your feeder often leads to a lifetime pursuit of bird identification. The *Birds of Nevada Field Guide* is for those who want to identify the common birds of Nevada.

There are over 1,100 species of birds found in North America. In Nevada alone there have been more than 490 different kinds of birds recorded throughout the years. These bird sightings were diligently recorded by hundreds of bird watchers and became part of the official state record. From these valuable records, I've chosen 139 of the most common birds of Nevada to include in this field guide.

Bird watching, often called birding, is one of the most popular activities in America. Its outstanding appeal in Nevada is due, in part, to an unusually rich and abundant birdlife. Why are there so many birds? One reason is open space. Nevada is more than 110,000 square miles (28,500 sq. km). It's the seventh largest state. Despite its size, only about 3.2 million people call Nevada home. On average, that is only 33 people per square mile (15 per sq. km).

Open space is not the only reason there is such an abundance of birds. It's also the diversity of habitat. Nevada lies nearly entirely in the Basin and Range Province, which is defined by mountain ranges oriented in a north-to-south pattern and with dramatic changes in between, resulting in many ranges and valleys (or basins). This dramatic topography provides habitat for a variety of birds.

Much of the northern part of the state is the Great Basin, which contains mild desert habitat that produces hot daytime temperatures in summer and very cold temperatures in winter.

Many open-country birds such as Ferruginous and Red-tailed Hawks live in this arid part of the state.

The state has many mountains, with two peaks reaching over 13,000 feet (4,000 m). The slopes of these mountains are habitat for thick evergreen forests, which are home to many bird species. The valleys in this region are often no lower than 3,000 to 6,000 feet (900–1,800 m). This part of the state is a great place to see alpine birds such as the Mountain Chickadee and Cassin's Finch.

The southern region of the state, where Las Vegas is found, is in the Mojave Desert. This part of the state receives very little rain in the winter but sometimes is on the receiving end of the Arizona Monsoons in summer. This region is mostly below 4,000 feet (1,200 m) in elevation and is extremely hot in summer and chilly in winter and is home to such birds as the Common Raven and Green-tailed Towhee.

Water also plays a large part in Nevada's bird populations. The Humboldt River stretches across the central portion of the state, from east to west. Several other rivers, such as the Walker, Truckee, and Carson Rivers, also run through the state. Parts of the Snake River, and the Colorado River, which forms much of the boundary with Arizona, flow through the state. They also attract a wide variety of birds such as several species of duck and Red-winged Blackbirds It's always worth time to investigate any body of water in Nevada for the presence of birds.

No matter if you are in the hot and dry basin lands or in the cool, moist mountains of Nevada, there are birds to watch in each season. Whether witnessing a migration of hawks in autumn or welcoming back hummingbirds in spring, there is variety and excitement in birding as each season turns to the next.

OBSERVE WITH A STRATEGY: TIPS FOR IDENTIFYING BIRDS

Identifying birds isn't as difficult as you might think. By simply following a few basic strategies, you can increase your chances of successfully identifying most birds that you see. One of the first and easiest things to do when you see a new bird is to note **its color.** This field guide is organized by color, so simply turn to the right color section to find it.

Next, note the **size of the bird.** A strategy to quickly estimate size is to compare different birds. Pick a small, a medium, and a large bird. Select an American Robin as the medium bird. Measured from bill tip to tail tip, a robin is 10 inches (25 cm). Now select two other birds, one smaller and one larger. Good choices are a House Sparrow, at about 6 inches (15 cm), and an American Crow, around 18 inches (45 cm). When you see a species you don't know, you can now quickly ask yourself, "Is it larger than a sparrow but smaller than a robin?" When you look in your field guide to identify your bird, you would check the species that are roughly 6–10 inches (15–25 cm). This will help to narrow your choices.

Next, note the **size, shape, and color of the bill.** Is it long or short, thick or thin, pointed or blunt, curved or straight? Seed-eating birds, such as Evening Grosbeaks, have bills that are thick and strong enough to crack even the toughest seeds. Birds that sip nectar, such as Black-chinned Hummingbirds, need long, thin bills to reach deep into flowers. Hawks and owls tear their prey with very sharp, curving bills. Sometimes, just noting the bill shape can help you decide whether the bird is a woodpecker, finch, grosbeak, blackbird, or bird of prey.

Next, take a look around and note the **habitat** in which you see the bird. Is it wading in a marsh? Walking along a riverbank or on the beach? Soaring in the sky? Is it perched high in the trees or hopping along the forest floor? Because of diet and habitat preferences, you'll often see robins hopping on the ground but not usually eating seeds at a feeder. Or you'll see a Black-headed Grosbeak sitting on a tree branch but not climbing headfirst down the trunk, like a Red-breasted Nuthatch would.

Noticing **what the bird is eating** will give you another clue to help you identify the species. Feeding is a big part of any bird's life. Fully one-third of all bird activity revolves around searching for food, catching prey and eating. While birds don't always follow all the rules of their diet, you can make some general assumptions. Northern Flickers, for instance, feed on ants and other insects, so you wouldn't expect to see them visiting a seed feeder. Other birds, such as Barn and Cliff Swallows, eat flying insects and spend hours swooping and diving to catch a meal.

Sometimes you can identify a bird by **the way it perches.** Body posture can help you differentiate between an American Crow and a Red-tailed Hawk, for example. Crows lean forward over their feet on a branch, while hawks perch in a vertical position. Consider posture the next time you see an unidentified large bird in a tree.

Birds in flight are harder to identify, but noting the **wing size and shape** will help. Wing size is in direct proportion to body size, weight and type of flight. Wing shape determines whether the bird flies fast and with precision, or slowly and less precisely. Barn Swallows, for instance, have short, pointed wings that slice through the air, enabling swift, accurate flight. Turkey Vultures have long, broad wings for soaring on warm updrafts. House Finches have short, rounded wings, helping them to flit through thick tangles of branches.

Some bird species have a unique **pattern of flight** that can help in identification. American Goldfinches fly in a distinctive undulating pattern that makes it look like they're riding a roller coaster.

While it's not easy to make all of these observations in the short time you often have to watch a "mystery" bird, practicing these identification methods will greatly expand your birding skills. To further improve your skills, seek the guidance of a more experienced birder who can answer your questions on the spot.

BIRD BASICS

It's easier to identify birds and communicate about them if you know the names of the different parts of a bird. For instance, it's more effective to use the word "crest" to indicate the set of extra-long feathers on top of a Steller's Jay head than to try to describe it.

The following illustration points out the basic parts of a bird. Because it is a composite of many birds, it shouldn't be confused with any actual bird.

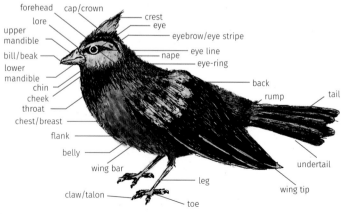

Bird Color Variables

No other animal has a color palette like a bird's. Brilliant blues, lemon yellows, showy reds, and iridescent greens are common in the bird world. In general, male birds are more colorful than their female counterparts. This helps males attract a mate, essentially saying, "Hey, look at me!" Color calls attention to a male's health as well. The better the condition of his feathers, the better his food source, territory, and potential for mating.

Male and female birds that don't look like each other are called sexually dimorphic, meaning "two forms." Dimorphic females often have a nondescript dull color, as seen in Lazuli Buntings. Muted tones help females hide during the weeks of motionless incubation and draw less attention to them when they're out feeding or taking a break from the rigors of raising the young.

The males of some species, such as the Hairy Woodpecker, Steller's Jay, and Bald Eagle, look nearly identical to the females. In woodpeckers, the sexes are differentiated by only a red mark, or sometimes a yellow mark. Depending on the species, the mark may be on top of the head, on the face or nape of neck, or just behind the bill.

During the first year, juvenile birds often look like their mothers. Since brightly colored feathers are used mainly for attracting a mate, young non-breeding males don't have a need for colorful plumage. It's not until the first spring molt (or several years later, depending on the species) that young males obtain their breeding colors.

Both breeding and winter plumages are the result of molting. Molting is the process of dropping old, worn feathers and replacing them with new ones. All birds molt, typically twice a year, with the spring molt usually occurring in late winter. At this time, most birds produce their brighter breeding plumage, which lasts throughout the summer.

Winter plumage is the result of the late summer molt, which serves a couple of important functions. First, it adds feathers for warmth in the coming winter season. Second, in some species it produces feathers that tend to be drab in color, which helps to camouflage the birds and hide them from predators. The winter plumage of the male American Goldfinch, for example, is olive-brown, unlike its canary-yellow breeding color during summer. Luckily for us, some birds, such as the male Lewis's Woodpeckers, retain their bright summer colors all year long.

Bird Nests

Bird nests are a true feat of engineering. Imagine constructing a home that's strong enough to weather storms, large enough to hold your entire family, insulated enough to shelter them from cold and heat, and waterproof enough to keep out rain. Think about building it without blueprints or directions and using mainly your feet. Birds do this!

Before building, birds must select an appropriate site. In some species, such as the House Wren, the male picks out several potential sites and assembles small twigs in each. The "extra" nests, called dummy nests, discourage other birds from using any nearby cavities for their nests. The male takes the female around and shows her the choices. After choosing her favorite, she finishes the construction.

In other species, such as the Bullock's Oriole, the female selects the site and builds the nest, while the male offers an occasional suggestion. Each bird species has its own nest-building routine that is strictly followed.

As you can see in the illustrations on the next page, birds build a wide variety of nest types.

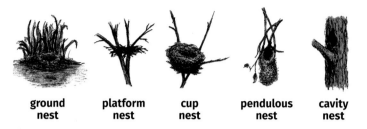

| ground nest | platform nest | cup nest | pendulous nest | cavity nest |

Nesting material often consists of natural items found in the immediate area. Most nests consist of plant fibers (such as bark from grapevines), sticks, mud, dried grass, feathers, fur, or soft, fuzzy tufts from thistle. Some birds, including Black-chinned Hummingbirds, use spiderwebs to glue nest materials together.

Transportation of nesting material is limited to the amount a bird can hold or carry. Birds must make many trips afield to gather enough material to complete a nest. Most nests take four days or more, and hundreds, if not thousands, of trips to build.

A **ground nest** can be a mound of vegetation on the ground or in the water. It can also be just a simple, shallow depression scraped out in earth, stones, or sand. Killdeer and Horned Larks scrape out ground nests without adding any nesting material.

The **platform nest** represents a much more complex type of construction. Typically built with twigs or sticks and branches, this nest forms a platform and has a depression in the center to nestle the eggs. Platform nests can be in trees; on balconies, cliffs, bridges, or man-made platforms; and even in flowerpots. They often provide space for the adventurous young and function as a landing platform for the parents.

Mourning Doves and herons don't anchor their platform nests to trees, so these can tumble from branches during high winds and storms. Hawks, eagles, and other birds construct sturdier platform nests with large sticks and branches.

Other platform nests are constructed on the ground with mud, grass, and other vegetation from the area. Many waterfowl build platform nests on the ground near or in water. A **floating platform nest** moves with the water level, preventing the nest, eggs, and birds from being flooded.

Three-quarters of all songbirds construct a **cup nest,** which is a modified platform nest. The supporting platform is built first and attached firmly to a tree, shrub, rock ledge, or the ground. Next, the sides are constructed with grass, small twigs, bark, or leaves, which are woven together and often glued with mud for added strength. The inner cup can be lined with down feathers, animal fur or hair, or soft plant materials and is contoured last.

The **pendulous nest** is an unusual nest that looks like a sock hanging from a branch. Attached to the end of small branches of trees, this unique nest is inaccessible to most predators and often waves wildly in a breeze.

Woven tightly with plant fibers, the pendulous nest is strong and watertight and takes up to a week to build. A small opening at the top or on the side allows parents access to the grass-lined interior. More commonly used by tropical birds, this complex nest has also been mastered by orioles and kinglets. It must be one heck of a ride to be inside one of these nests during a windy spring thunderstorm!

The **cavity nest** is used by many species of birds, most notably woodpeckers and Western Bluebirds. A cavity nest is often excavated from a branch or tree trunk and offers shelter from storms, sun, cold, and predators. A small entrance hole in a tree can lead to a nest chamber that is up to a safe 10 inches (25 cm) deep.

Typically made by woodpeckers, cavity nests are usually used only once by the builder. Nest cavities can be used for many subsequent years by such inhabitants as Tree Swallows, mergansers, and bluebirds. Kingfishers, on the other hand, can dig a tunnel up to 4 feet (about 1 m) long in a riverbank. The nest chamber at the end of the tunnel is already well insulated, so it's usually only sparsely lined.

One of the most clever of all nests is the **no nest,** or daycare nest. Parasitic birds, such as Brown-headed Cowbirds, don't build their own nests. Instead, the egg-laden female searches out the nest of another bird and sneaks in to lay an egg while the host mother isn't looking.

A mother cowbird wastes no energy building a nest only to have it raided by a predator. Laying her eggs in the nests of other birds transfers the responsibility of raising her young to the host. When she lays her eggs in several nests, the chances increase that at least one of her babies will live to maturity.

Who Builds the Nest?

Generally, the female bird constructs the nest. She gathers the materials and does the building, with an occasional visit from her mate to check on progress. In some species, both parents contribute equally to nest building. The male may forage for sticks, grass, or mud, but it is the female that often fashions the nest. Only rarely does a male build a nest by himself.

Fledging

Fledging is the time between hatching and flight, or leaving the nest. Some species of birds are **precocial,** meaning they leave the nest within hours of hatching, though it may be weeks before they can fly. This is common in waterfowl and shorebirds.

Baby birds that hatch naked and blind need to stay in the nest for a few weeks (these birds are **altricial**). Baby birds that are still in the nest are **nestlings.** Until birds start to fly, they are called **fledglings.**

Why Birds Migrate

Why do so many species of birds migrate? The short answer is simple: food. Birds migrate to locations with abundant food, as it is easier to breed where there is food than where food is scarce. Western Tanagers, for instance, are **complete migrators** that fly from the tropics of South America to nest in the forests of North America, where billions of newly hatched insects are available to feed to their young.

Other migrators, such as some birds of prey, migrate back to northern regions in spring. In these locations, they hunt mice, voles and other small rodents that are beginning to breed.

Complete migrators have a set time and pattern of migration. Every year at nearly the same time, they head to a specific wintering ground. Complete migrators may travel great distances, sometimes 15,000 miles (24,100 km) or more in one year.

Complete migration doesn't necessarily imply flying from the cold, frozen northland to a tropical destination. The White-throated Swift, for example, is a complete migrator that flies from Nevada to Mexico and Central America. This trip is still considered complete migration.

Complete migrators have many interesting aspects. In spring, males often leave a few weeks before the females, arriving early to scope out possibilities for nesting sites and food sources, and to begin to defend territories. The females arrive several weeks later. In many species, the females and their young leave earlier in the fall, often up to four weeks before the adult males.

Other species, such as the American Goldfinch, are **partial migrators**. These birds usually wait until their food supplies dwindle before flying south. Unlike complete migrators, partial migrators move only far enough south, or sometimes east and west, to find abundant food. In some years it might be only a few hundred miles, while in other years it can be as much as a thousand. This kind of migration, dependent on weather and the availability of food, is sometimes called seasonal movement.

Unlike the predictable complete migrators or partial migrators, **irruptive migrators** can move every third to fifth year or, in some cases, in consecutive years. These migrations are triggered when times are tough and food is scarce. Red-breasted Nuthatches are irruptive migrators. They leave their normal northern range in search of more food or in response to overpopulation.

Many other birds don't migrate at all. Mountain Chickadees, for example, are **non-migrators** that remain in their habitat all year long and just move around as necessary to find food.

How Do Birds Migrate?

One of the many secrets of migration is fat. While most people are fighting the ongoing battle of the bulge, birds intentionally gorge themselves to gain as much fat as possible without losing the ability to fly. Fat provides the greatest amount of energy per unit of weight. In the same way that your car needs gas, birds are propelled by fat and stall without it.

During long migratory flights, fat deposits are used up quickly, and birds need to stop to refuel. This is when backyard bird feeding stations and undeveloped, natural spaces around our towns and cities are especially important. Some birds require up to 2–3 days of constant feeding to build their fat reserves before continuing their seasonal trip.

Many birds, such as most eagles, hawks, falcons, and vultures, migrate during the day. Larger birds can hold more body fat, go longer without eating, and take longer to migrate. These birds glide along on rising columns of warm air, called thermals, that hold them aloft while they slowly make their way north or south. They generally rest at night and hunt early in the morning before the sun has a chance to warm the land and create good soaring conditions. Daytime migrators use a combination of landforms, rivers, and the rising and setting sun to guide them in the right direction.

The majority of small birds, called **passerines,** migrate at night. Studies show that some use the stars to navigate. Others use the setting sun, and still others, such as pigeons, use Earth's magnetic field to guide them north or south.

While flying at night may not seem like a good idea, it's actually safer. First, there are fewer avian predators hunting for birds at night. Second, night travel allows time during the day to find food in unfamiliar surroundings. Third, wind patterns at night tend to be flat, or laminar. Flat winds don't have the turbulence of daytime winds and can help push the smaller birds along.

HOW TO USE THIS GUIDE

To help you quickly and easily identify birds, this field guide is organized by color. Refer to the color key on the first page, note the color of the bird, and turn to that section. For example, the Williamson's Sapsucker is black and white with a yellow belly. Because the bird is mostly black-and-white, it will be found in the black-and-white section.

Each color section is also arranged by size, generally with the smaller birds first. Sections may also incorporate the average size in a range, which in some cases reflects size differences between male and female birds. Flip through the pages in the color section to find the bird. If you already know the name of the bird, check the index for the page number.

In some species, the male and female are very different in color. In others, the breeding and winter plumage colors differ. These species will have an inset photograph with a page reference and will be found in two color sections.

You will find a variety of information in the bird description sections. To learn more, turn to the sample on pp. 22–23.

Range Maps

Range maps are included for each bird. Colored areas indicate where the bird is frequently found. The colors represent the presence of a species during a specific season, not the density, or amount, of birds in the area. Green is used for summer, blue for winter, red for year-round, and yellow for migration.

While every effort has been made to depict accurate ranges, these are constantly in flux due to a variety of factors. Changing weather, habitat, species abundance, and availability of vital resources, such as food and water, can affect the migration and movement of local populations, causing birds to be found in areas that are atypical for the species. So please use the maps as intended—as general guides only.

female
p. 335

male

Common Name

Scientific name

YEAR-ROUND
SUMMER
MIGRATION
WINTER

Size: measurement is from head to tip of tail; wingspan may be listed as well

Male: brief description of the male bird; may include breeding, winter, or other plumages

Female: brief description of the female bird, which is sometimes different from the male

Juvenile: brief description of the juvenile bird, which often looks like the adult female

Nest: kind of nest the bird builds to raise its young; who builds it; number of broods per year

Eggs: number of eggs you might expect to see in a nest; color and marking

Incubation: average days the parents spend incubating the eggs; who does the incubation

Fledging: average days the young spend in the nest after hatching but before they leave the nest; who does the most "childcare" and feeding

Migration: type of migrator: complete (seasonal, consistent), partial (seasonal, destination varies), irruptive (unpredictable, depends on the food supply) or non-migrator

Food: what the bird eats most of the time (e.g., seeds, insects, fruit, nectar, small mammals, fish) and whether it typically comes to a bird feeder

Compare: notes about other birds that look similar and the pages on which they can be found; may include extra information to aid in identification

Stan's Notes: Interesting natural history information. This could be something to look or listen for or something to help positively identify the bird. Also includes remarkable features.

female
p. 129

male

Brown-headed Cowbird
Molothrus ater

YEAR-ROUND
SUMMER

Size: 7½" (19 cm)

Male: Glossy black with a chocolate-brown head. Dark eyes. Pointed, sharp gray bill.

Female: dull brown with a pointed, sharp gray bill

Juvenile: similar to female but with dull-gray plumage and a streaked chest

Nest: no nest; lays eggs in nests of other birds

Eggs: 5–7; white with brown markings

Incubation: 10–13 days; host birds incubate eggs

Fledging: 10–11 days; host birds feed the young

Migration: complete, to Arizona and New Mexico; non-migrator in parts of the state

Food: insects, seeds; will come to seed feeders

Compare: The male Red-winged Blackbird (p. 29) is slightly larger with red-and-yellow patches on upper wings. European Starling (p. 25) has a shorter tail.

Stan's Notes: Cowbirds are members of the blackbird family. Of approximately 750 species of parasitic birds worldwide, this is the only parasitic bird in Nevada. Brood parasites lay their eggs in the nests of other birds, leaving the host birds to raise their young. Cowbirds are known to have laid their eggs in the nests of over 200 species of birds. While some birds reject cowbird eggs, most incubate them and raise the young, even to the exclusion of their own. Look for warblers and other birds feeding young birds twice their own size. Named "Cowbird" for its habit of following bison and cattle herds to feed on insects flushed up by the animals.

winter

breeding

European Starling
Sturnus vulgaris

YEAR-ROUND

Size:	7½" (19 cm)
Male:	Glittering, iridescent purplish black in spring and summer; duller and speckled with white in fall and winter. Long, pointed, yellow bill in spring; gray in fall. Pointed wings. Short tail.
Female:	same as male
Juvenile:	similar to adults, with grayish-brown plumage and a streaked chest
Nest:	cavity; male and female line cavity; 2 broods per year
Eggs:	4–6; bluish without markings
Incubation:	12–14 days; female and male incubate
Fledging:	18–20 days; female and male feed the young
Migration:	non-migrator to partial migrator; some will move to southern states; moves around to find food
Food:	insects, seeds, fruit; visits seed or suet feeders
Compare:	The male Brown-headed Cowbird (p. 23) has a brown head. Look for the shiny, dark feathers to help identify the European Starling.

Stan's Notes: One of our most numerous songbirds. Mimics the songs of up to 20 bird species and imitates sounds, including the human voice. Jaws are more powerful when opening than when closing, enabling the bird to pry open crevices to find insects. Often displaces woodpeckers, chickadees, and other cavity-nesting birds. Large families gather with blackbirds in the fall. Not a native bird; 100 starlings were introduced to New York City in 1890–91 from Europe. Bill changes color in spring and fall.

Spotted Towhee
Pipilo maculatus

YEAR-ROUND

Size: 8½" (22 cm)

Male: Mostly black with dirty red-brown sides and a white belly. Multiple white spots on wings and sides. Long black tail with a white tip. Rich, red eyes.

Female: very similar to male but with a brown head

Juvenile: brown with a heavily streaked chest

Nest: cup; female builds; 1–2 broods per year

Eggs: 3–5; white with brown markings

Incubation: 12–14 days; female incubates

Fledging: 10–12 days; female and male feed young

Migration: partial to non-migrator; moves around to find food

Food: seeds, fruit, insects

Compare: Closely related to the Green-tailed Towhee (p. 293), which lacks the bold black and red colors. American Robin (p. 251) is larger.

Stan's Notes: Not as common as the Green-tailed Towhee, but it inhabits similar habitat. Mostly found from 5,000 to 7,000 feet (1,500 to 2,150 m) of elevation in oak scrub country. Usually heard noisily scratching through dead leaves on the ground for food. Over 70 percent of its diet is plant material. Eats more insects during spring and summer. Well known to retreat from danger by walking away rather than taking to flight. Nest is nearly always on the ground under bushes but away from where the male perches to sing. Begins breeding in April. Lays eggs in May. After the breeding season, moves to higher elevations. Song and plumage vary geographically and aren't well studied or understood.

female
p. 137

male

Red-winged Blackbird
Agelaius phoeniceus

YEAR-ROUND

Size: 8½" (22 cm)

Male: Jet black with red-and-yellow patches (epaulets) on upper wings. Pointed black bill.

Female: heavily streaked brown with a pointed brown bill and white eyebrows

Juvenile: same as female

Nest: cup; female builds; 2–3 broods per year

Eggs: 3–4; bluish green with brown markings

Incubation: 10–12 days; female incubates

Fledging: 11–14 days; female and male feed the young

Migration: non-migrator to partial; will move around the state to find food in winter

Food: seeds, insects; visits seed feeders

Compare: The male Brown-headed Cowbird (p. 23) is smaller and glossier and has a brown head. The bold red-and-yellow epaulets distinguish the male Red-winged from other blackbirds.

Stan's Notes: One of the most widespread and numerous birds in Nevada. Found around marshes, wetlands, lakes, and rivers. Flocks with as many as 10,000 birds have been reported. Males arrive before the females and sing to defend their territory. The male repeats his call from the top of a cattail while showing off his red-and-yellow shoulder patches. The female chooses a mate and often builds her nest over shallow water in a thick stand of cattails. The male can be aggressive when defending the nest. Red-winged Blackbirds feed mostly on seeds in spring and fall, and insects throughout the summer.

female
p. 139

male

Brewer's Blackbird
Euphagus cyanocephalus

YEAR-ROUND
WINTER

Size: 9" (22.5 cm)

Male: Overall glossy black, shining green in direct light. Head more purple than green. Bright-white or pale-yellow eyes. Winter plumage can be dull gray to black.

Female: similar to male, only overall grayish brown, most have dark eyes

Juvenile: similar to female

Nest: cup; female builds; 1–2 broods per year

Eggs: 4–6; gray with brown markings

Incubation: 12–14 days; female incubates

Fledging: 13–14 days; female and male feed young

Migration: non-migrator to partial migrator in Nevada

Food: insects, seeds, fruit

Compare: Smaller than the male Great-tailed Grackle (p. 37), lacking the long tail. The male Brown-headed Cowbird (p. 23) is smaller and has a brown head. Male Red-winged Blackbird (p. 29) has red and yellow shoulder marks.

Stan's Notes: Common blackbird often found in association with agricultural lands and seen in open areas such as wet pastures, mountain meadows up to 10,000 feet (3,050 m), and even desert scrub. Male and some females are easily identified by their bright, nearly white eyes. It is a common cowbird host, usually nesting in a shrub, small tree, or directly on the ground. Prefers to nest in small colonies of up to 20 pairs. Gathers in large flocks with cowbirds, Red-wingeds, and other blackbirds to migrate. It is expanding its range in North America.

female
p. 147

male

Yellow-headed Blackbird
Xanthocephalus xanthocephalus

**YEAR-ROUND
SUMMER**

Size: 9–11" (23–28 cm)

Male: Large black bird with a lemon-yellow head, breast, and nape of neck. Black mask and gray bill. White wing patches.

Female: similar to male but slightly smaller with a brown body and dull-yellow head and chest

Juvenile: similar to female

Nest: cup; female builds; 1–2 broods per year

Eggs: 3–5; greenish white with brown markings

Incubation: 11–13 days; female incubates

Fledging: 9–12 days; female and male feed the young

Migration: complete, to Arizona, New Mexico, and Mexico

Food: insects, seeds; will come to ground feeders

Compare: The male Red-winged Blackbird (p. 29) is smaller and has red-and-yellow patches on its wings. Look for the bright-yellow head to identify the male Yellow-headed.

Stan's Notes: Found around marshes, wetlands, and lakes. Nests in deep water, unlike its cousin, the Red-winged Blackbird, which prefers shallow water. Usually heard before seen. Gives a raspy, low, metallic-sounding call. The male is the only large blackbird with a bright-yellow head. He gives an impressive mating display, flying with his head drooped and feet and tail pointing down while steadily beating his wings. Young keep low and out of sight for up to three weeks before they start to fly. Migrates in large flocks of as many as 200 birds, often with Red-winged Blackbirds and Brown-headed Cowbirds. Flocks of mainly males return in first; females return later. Most colonies consist of 20–100 nests.

American Coot
Fulica americana

YEAR-ROUND

Size: 13–16" (33–40 cm)

Male: Gray-to-black waterbird. Duck-like white bill with a dark band near the tip and a small red patch near the eyes. Small white patch near base of tail. Green legs and feet. Red eyes.

Female: same as male

Juvenile: much paler than adults, with a gray bill

Nest: floating platform; female and male construct; 1–2 broods per year

Eggs: 9–12; pinkish buff with brown markings

Incubation: 21–25 days; female and male incubate

Fledging: 49–52 days; female and male feed young

Migration: non-migrator to partial migrator in Nevada

Food: insects, aquatic plants

Compare: Smaller than most waterfowl, it is the only black, duck-like bird with a white bill.

Stan's Notes: Usually seen in large flocks on open water. Not a duck, as it has large lobed toes instead of webbed feet. An excellent diver and swimmer, bobbing its head as it swims. A favorite food of Bald Eagles. It is not often seen in flight, unless it's trying to escape from an eagle. To take off, it scrambles across the surface of the water, flapping its wings. Gives a unique series of creaks, groans, and clicks. Anchors its floating platform nest to vegetation. Huge flocks with as many as 1,000 birds gather for migration. Migrates at night. The common name "Coot" comes from the Middle English word *coote*, which was used to describe various waterfowl. Also called Mud Hen.

female
p. 161

male

Great-tailed Grackle
Quiscalus mexicanus

YEAR-ROUND
SUMMER

Size: 18" (45 cm), male
15" (38 cm), female

Male: Large all-black bird with iridescent purple sheen on the head and back. Exceptionally long tail. Bright-yellow eyes.

Female: considerably smaller than the male, overall brown bird with gray-to-brown belly, light-brown-to-white eyes, eyebrows, throat, and upper chest

Juvenile: similar to female

Nest: cup; female builds; 1–2 broods per year

Eggs: 3–5; greenish blue with brown markings

Incubation: 12–14 days; female incubates

Fledging: 21–23 days; female feeds young

Migration: partial migrator; will move around to find food; non-migrator in parts of Nevada

Food: insects, fruit, seeds; comes to seed feeders

Compare: Male Brown-headed Cowbird (p. 23) lacks the long tail and has a brown head.

Stan's Notes: This is our largest grackle. It was once considered a subspecies of the Boat-tailed Grackle, which occurs along the East Coast and Florida. A bird that prefers to nest near water in an open habitat. A colony nester. Males do not participate in nest building, incubation, or raising young. Males rarely fight; females squabble over nest sites and materials. Several females mate with one male. They are expanding northward, moving into northern states. Western populations tend to be larger than the eastern. Song varies from population to population.

in flight

American Crow
Corvus brachyrhynchos

YEAR-ROUND
WINTER

Size: 18" (45 cm)

Male: All-black bird with black bill, legs, and feet. Can have a purple sheen in direct sunlight.

Female: same as male

Juvenile: same as adult

Nest: platform; female and male build; 1 brood per year

Eggs: 4–6; bluish to olive-green with brown marks

Incubation: 18 days; female incubates

Fledging: 28–35 days; female and male feed the young

Migration: non-migrator to partial migrator

Food: fruit, insects, mammals, fish, carrion; will come to seed and suet feeders

Compare: Common Raven (p. 41) is similar, but it has a larger bill and has shaggy throat feathers. Crow's call is higher than the raspy, low calls of the raven. Crow has a squared tail. Raven has a wedge-shaped tail, apparent in flight. Black-billed Magpie (p. 63) has a long tail and white belly.

Stan's Notes: One of the most recognizable birds in Nevada, found in most habitats. Imitates other birds and human voices. One of the smartest of all birds and very social, often entertaining itself by provoking chases with other birds. Eats roadkill but is rarely hit by vehicles. Can live as long as 20 years. Often reuses its nest every year if it's not taken over by a Great Horned Owl. Unmated birds, known as helpers, help to raise the young. Extended families roost together at night, dispersing daily to hunt. Cannot soar on thermals; flaps constantly and glides downward. Gathers in huge communal flocks of up to 10,000 birds in winter.

in flight

Common Raven
Corvus corax

YEAR-ROUND

Size: 22–27" (56–69 cm)

Male: Large all-black bird with a shaggy beard of feathers on throat and chin. Large black bill. Large wedge-shaped tail, best seen in flight.

Female: same as male

Juvenile: same as adult

Nest: platform; female and male construct; 1 brood per year

Eggs: 4–6; pale green with brown markings

Incubation: 18–21 days; female incubates

Fledging: 38–44 days; female and male feed the young

Migration: non-migrator to partial migrator, moves around to find food

Food: insects, fruit, small animals, carrion

Compare: American Crow (p. 39) is smaller and lacks the shaggy throat feathers. Low raspy call, compared with the higher-pitched call of the American Crow.

Stan's Notes: Considered by some people to be the smartest of all birds. Known for its aerial acrobatics and long swooping dives. Soars on wind without flapping, like a raptor. Sometimes scavenges with crows and gulls. A cooperative hunter that often communicates the location of a good source of food to other ravens. Most start to breed at 3–4 years. Complex courtship includes grabbing bills, preening each other, and cooing. Long-term pair bond. Uses the same nest site for many years.

soaring

juvenile

drying

SUMMER

Turkey Vulture
Cathartes aura

Size: 26–32" (66–80 cm); up to 6' wingspan

Male: Large and black with a naked red head and legs. In flight, wings are two-toned with a black leading edge and a gray trailing edge. Wing tips end in finger-like projections. Tail is long and squared. Ivory bill.

Female: same as male but slightly smaller

Juvenile: similar to adults, with a gray-to-blackish head and bill

Nest: no nest or minimal nest, on a cliff or in a cave, sometimes in a hollow tree; 1 brood per year

Eggs: 1–3; white with brown markings

Incubation: 38–41 days; female and male incubate

Fledging: 66–88 days; female and male feed the young

Migration: complete, to Arizona, Texas, Mexico, Central America, and South America

Food: carrion; parents regurgitate to feed the young

Compare: Bald Eagle (p. 69) is larger and lacks two-toned wings. Look for the obvious naked red head to identify the Turkey Vulture.

Stan's Notes: The naked head reduces the risk of feather fouling (picking up diseases) from contact with carcasses. It has a strong bill for tearing apart flesh. Unlike hawks and eagles, it has weak feet more suited for walking than grasping. One of the few birds with a developed sense of smell. Mostly mute, making only grunts and groans. Holds its wings in an upright V shape in flight. Teeters from wing tip to wing tip as it soars and hovers. Seen in trees with wings outstretched, sunning itself and drying after a rain.

White-throated Swift

Aeronautes saxatalis

YEAR-ROUND
SUMMER

Size: 6½" (16 cm)

Male: Black with a white chin, chest, and sides of rump. White trailing edge on the length of the first half of wings. Long narrow wings and long thin tail, as seen in flight.

Female: same as male

Juvenile: similar to adult

Nest: cup, in a cavity or crevice; female and male build; 1 brood per year

Eggs: 4–5; white without markings

Incubation: 20–27; female and male incubate

Fledging: unknown days; female and male feed the young

Migration: complete, to Arizona, New Mexico, Mexico, and Central America

Food: insects

Compare: Similar (but not related) to the Violet-green Swallow (p. 291), which is entirely white beneath, compared with the narrow white band on the belly of White-throated Swift.

Stan's Notes: A common bird of rocky canyons in elevations from 5,500 to 8,200 feet (1,700 to 2,500 m). A perpetual flyer, it feeds, bathes, and even mates while flying. Pairs press together and spin down through air, then break apart. Flies in groups, giving twittering calls. Returns in April. Doesn't nest until summer, when more insects are available to feed to young. Carries food to the young in an expandable throat pouch. Nests in small colonies, constructing cup-shaped nests in rock crevices. Like other swifts, uses its saliva to glue feathers and vegetation into a cup that it seals to the rock.

male

female

Downy Woodpecker
Dryobates pubescens

YEAR-ROUND

Size: 6½" (15 cm)

Male: Small woodpecker with a white belly and black-and-white spotted wings. Red mark on the back of the head and a white stripe down the back. Short black bill.

Female: same as male but lacks the red mark

Juvenile: same as female, some with a red mark near the forehead

Nest: cavity with a round entrance hole; male and female excavate; 1 brood per year

Eggs: 3–5; white without markings

Incubation: 11–12 days; female incubates during the day, male incubates at night

Fledging: 20–25 days; male and female feed the young

Migration: non-migrator

Food: insects, seeds; visits seed and suet feeders

Compare: The Hairy Woodpecker (p. 49) is larger. Look for the Downy's shorter, thinner bill.

Stan's Notes: This is perhaps the most common woodpecker in the US. Stiff tail feathers help to brace it like a tripod as it clings to a tree. Like other woodpeckers, it has a long, barbed tongue to pull insects from tiny places. Mates drum on branches or hollow logs to announce territory. Repeats a high-pitched "peek-peek" call. Male performs most of the brooding. During winter, it will roost in a cavity. Doesn't breed in high elevations but often moves there in winter for food. Undulates in flight.

male

female

YEAR-ROUND

Hairy Woodpecker
Leuconotopicus villosus

Size: 9" (23 cm)

Male: Black-and-white woodpecker with a white belly. Black wings with rows of white spots. White stripe down the back. Long black bill. Red mark on the back of the head.

Female: same as male but lacks the red mark

Juvenile: grayer version of the female

Nest: cavity with an oval entrance hole; female and male excavate; 1 brood per year

Eggs: 3–6; white without markings

Incubation: 11–15 days; female incubates during the day, male incubates at night

Fledging: 28–30 days; male and female feed the young

Migration: non-migrator; moves around in winter to find food

Food: insects, nuts, seeds; comes to seed and suet feeders

Compare: Downy Woodpecker (p. 47) is much smaller and has a much shorter bill. Look for Hairy Woodpecker's long bill.

Stan's Notes: A common bird in wooded backyards. Announces its arrival with a sharp chirp before landing on feeders. Responsible for eating many destructive forest insects. Uses its barbed tongue to extract insects from trees. Tiny, bristle-like feathers at the base of the bill protect the nostrils from wood dust. Drums on hollow logs, branches, or stovepipes in spring to announce territory. Prefers to excavate nest cavities in live aspen trees. Excavates a larger, more oval-shaped entrance than the round entrance hole of the Downy Woodpecker. Makes short flights from tree to tree.

male

female

Williamson's Sapsucker
Sphyrapicus thyroideus

YEAR-ROUND
SUMMER

Size: 9" (22.5 cm)

Male: More black than white with a red chin and bright-yellow belly. Bold white stripes just above and below the eyes. White rump and wing patches flash during flight.

Female: finely barred black-and-white back, a brown head, yellow belly, and no wing patches

Juvenile: similar to female

Nest: cavity; male excavates; 1 brood per year

Eggs: 3–7; pale white without markings

Incubation: 12–14 days; male and female incubate

Fledging: 21–28 days; female and male feed young

Migration: complete, to Mexico and Central America

Food: insects, tree sap; will visit feeders

Compare: Lewis's Woodpecker (p. 295) has a red face and belly. Female Williamson's is similar to the Northern Flicker (p. 151), but Flicker has a gray head and brown-and-black back.

Stan's Notes: Largest sapsucker species with a striking difference between the male and female. Male drums early in spring to attract a mate and claim territory. Like the drumming of other sapsuckers, Williamson's drumming has an irregular cadence. Male excavates a new cavity each year, frequently in the same tree. Male does more incubating than the female. Occupies coniferous forests, foraging for insects and drilling uniform rows of holes from which tree sap oozes.

female
p. 157

male

Bufflehead

Bucephala albeola

WINTER

Size: 13–15" (33–38 cm)

Male: A small, striking duck with white sides and a black back. Greenish-purple head, iridescent in bright sun, with a large white head patch.

Female: brownish-gray with a dark brown head and white cheek patch behind the eyes

Juvenile: similar to female

Nest: cavity; female lines an old woodpecker cavity; 1 brood per year

Eggs: 8–10; ivory-to-olive without markings

Incubation: 29–31 days; female incubates

Fledging: 50–55 days; female leads the young to food

Migration: complete, to Nevada, Arizona, and New Mexico

Food: aquatic insects, crustaceans, mollusks

Compare: The male Common Goldeneye (p. 59) is slightly larger, shares the white sides and black back, but lacks the white head patch. Look for the large white bonnet-like patch on a greenish-purple head to help identify the male Bufflehead.

Stan's Notes: A small, common diving duck, almost always seen in small groups or with other duck species on rivers, ponds, and lakes. Nests in vacant woodpecker holes. When cavities in trees are scarce, known to use a burrow in an earthen bank or will use a nest box. Lines the cavity with fluffy down feathers. Unlike other ducks, the young stay in the nest for up to two days before they venture out with their mothers. The female is very territorial and remains with the same mate for many years.

female p. 173

male

Lesser Scaup
Aythya affinis

YEAR-ROUND
MIGRATION
WINTER

Size: 16–17" (40–43 cm)

Male: Appears mostly black with bold white sides and a gray back. Chest and head look nearly black, but head appears purple with green highlights in direct sun. Bright-yellow eyes.

Female: overall brown with a dull-white patch at the base of a light-gray bill; yellow eyes

Juvenile: same as female

Nest: ground; female builds; 1 brood per year

Eggs: 8–14; olive-buff without markings

Incubation: 22–28 days; female incubates

Fledging: 45–50 days; female teaches the young to feed

Migration: complete, to California, Arizona, New Mexico, Texas, and Mexico

Food: aquatic plants and insects

Compare: The male Ring-necked Duck (p. 57) has a bold white ring around its bill, a black back and lacks the bold white sides of the male Lesser Scaup. The male Blue-winged Teal (p. 169) is slightly smaller and has a bright white crescent-shaped mark at base of bill.

Stan's Notes: A common diving duck. Often seen in large flocks on lakes, ponds and sewage lagoons. Submerges completely to feed on the bottom (unlike dabbling ducks, which tip forward to reach the bottom). The male leaves the female when she starts incubating eggs. Egg quantity (clutch size) increases with the female's age. Has an interesting babysitting arrangement: groups of young (crèches) are tended by one to three adult females.

female
p. 177

male

Ring-necked Duck

Aythya collaris

YEAR-ROUND
WINTER

Size: 16–19" (41–48 cm)

Male: Striking black duck with light-gray-to-white sides. Blue bill with a bold white ring and a thinner ring at the base. Peaked head with a sloped forehead.

Female: brown with darker-brown back and crown, light-brown sides, gray face, white eye-ring, white ring around the bill, and peaked head

Juvenile: similar to female

Nest: ground; female builds; 1 brood per year

Eggs: 8–10; olive-gray to brown without markings

Incubation: 26–27 days; female incubates

Fledging: 49–56 days; female teaches the young to feed

Migration: complete, to Nevada and southwestern states; non-migrator in parts of the state

Food: aquatic plants and insects

Compare: Look for the blue bill with a bold white ring to identify the male Ring-necked Duck.

Stan's Notes: Usually in larger freshwater lakes rather than saltwater marshes, in small flocks or just pairs. Watch for this diving duck to dive underwater to forage for food. Springs up off the water to take flight. Flattens its crown when diving. Male gives a quick series of grating barks and grunts. Female gives high-pitched peeps. Named "Ring-necked" for its cinnamon collar, which is nearly impossible to see in the field. Also called Ring-billed Duck due to the white ring on its bill.

female
p. 181

male

WINTER

Common Goldeneye
Bucephala clangula

Size: 18–20" (45–51 cm)

Male: Mostly white duck with a black back and a large, puffy, green head. Large white spot on the face. Bright-golden eyes. Dark bill.

Female: large dark-brown head with a gray body and a white collar, bright-golden eyes, yellow-tipped dark bill

Juvenile: same as female but has dark eyes

Nest: cavity; female lines an old woodpecker cavity; 1 brood per year

Eggs: 8–10; bluish to olive green without markings

Incubation: 28–32 days; female incubates

Fledging: 56–59 days; female leads the young to food

Migration: complete, to Nevada, other southwestern states, and Mexico

Food: aquatic plants, insects, fish, mollusks

Compare: Larger than American Coot (p. 35), which lacks the bright-golden eyes and white spot in front of each eye.

Stan's Notes: Known for the loud whistling sound produced by its wings during flight. During late winter and early spring, the male performs elaborate mating displays that include throwing his head back and calling a raspy note. The female will lay some of her eggs in other goldeneye nests or in the nests of other species (called egg dumping), causing some mothers to incubate as many as 30 eggs in a brood. Named for its bright-golden eyes. Winters in Nevada where it finds open water.

winter

breeding

SUMMER
MIGRATION

American Avocet
Recurvirostra americana

Size: 18" (45 cm)

Male: Black-and-white back, with a white belly. A long, thin upturned bill and long gray legs. Rusty-red head and neck during breeding season, gray in winter.

Female: similar to male, more strongly upturned bill

Juvenile: similar to adults, slight wash of rusty red on the neck and head

Nest: ground; female and male construct; 1 brood per year

Eggs: 3–5; light olive with brown markings

Incubation: 22–29 days; female and male incubate

Fledging: 28–35 days; female and male feed young

Migration: complete, to southern California and Mexico

Food: insects, crustaceans, aquatic vegetation

Compare: One of the few long-legged shorebirds in Nevada. Look for the rusty-red head of breeding Avocet and the long upturned bill.

Stan's Notes: A handsome, long-legged bird that prefers shallow alkaline, saline, or brackish water, it is well adapted to arid western US conditions. Uses its upturned bill to sweep from side to side across mud bottoms in search of insects. Both the male and female have a brood patch to incubate eggs and brood their young. Nests in loose colonies of up to 20 pairs; all members defend against intruders together.

Black-billed Magpie

Pica hudsonia

YEAR-ROUND

Size: 20" (50 cm)

Male: Large black-and-white bird with a very long tail and white belly. Iridescent green wings and tail in direct sunlight. Large black bill. Black legs. White wing patches flash in flight.

Female: same as male

Juvenile: same as adult, but has a shorter tail

Nest: modified pendulous; male and female build; 1 brood per year

Eggs: 5–8; green with brown markings

Incubation: 16–21 days; female incubates

Fledging: 25–29 days; female and male feed young

Migration: non-migrator

Food: insects, carrion, fruit, seeds

Compare: The contrasting black-and-white colors and the very long tail of the Black-billed Magpie distinguish it from the all-black American Crow (p. 39).

Stan's Notes: A wonderfully intelligent bird that is able to mimic dogs, cats, and even people. Will often raid a barnyard dog dish for food. Feeds on a variety of food from roadkill to insects and seeds it collects from the ground. Easily identified by its bold black-and-white colors and long streaming tail. Travels in small flocks, usually family members, and tends to be very gregarious. Breeds in small colonies. Unusual dome nest (dome-shaped roof) deep within thick shrubs. Mates with same mate for several years. Prefers open fields with cattle or sheep, where it feeds on insects attracted to livestock.

in flight

juvenile

Black-crowned Night-Heron
Nycticorax nycticorax

Size: 22–27" (56–69 cm); up to 3½' wingspan

Male: A stocky, hunched, and inactive heron with black back and crown, white belly, and gray wings. Long dark bill and bright-red eyes. Short dull-yellow legs. Breeding adult has 2 long white plumes on crown.

Female: same as male

Juvenile: golden-brown head and back with white spots, streaked breast, yellow-orange eyes, brown bill

Nest: platform; female and male build; 1 brood per year

Eggs: 3–5; light greenish blue without markings

Incubation: 24–26 days; female and male incubate

Fledging: 42–48 days; female and male feed the young

Migration: complete, to the Southwest, Mexico, and Central America; non-migrator in parts of Nevada

Food: fish, aquatic insects

Compare: American Bittern (p. 209) is overall brown and has a yellow bill. Perching Great Blue Heron (p. 281) looks twice the size of a Black-crowned. Look for a short-necked heron with a black back and crown.

Stan's Notes: A very secretive bird, this heron is most active near dawn and dusk (crepuscular). It hunts alone, but it nests in small colonies. Roosts in trees during the day. Often squawks if disturbed from the daytime roost. Often seen being harassed by other herons during days. Stalks quiet backwaters in search of small fish and crabs.

rushing

weed dance

SUMMER

Western Grebe
Aechmophorus occidentalis

Size: 24" (60 cm)

Male: Long-necked, nearly all-black waterbird. White chin, neck, chest, and belly. Long greenish yellow bill. Bright-red eyes. Dark crown extends around eyes to base of bill. In winter, becomes light gray around eyes.

Female: same as male

Juvenile: similar to adult

Nest: floating platform; female and male construct; 1 brood per year

Eggs: 3–4; bluish white without markings

Incubation: 20–23 days; female and male incubate

Fledging: 65–75 days; female and male feed young

Migration: complete, to coastal California and Mexico

Food: fish, aquatic insects

Compare: A familiar long-necked waterbird. Striking black-and-white plumage makes it hard to confuse with any other bird.

Stan's Notes: Well known for its unusual breeding dance, called rushing. Side by side with necks outstretched, mates spring to their webbed feet and dance across the water's surface (see inset). Often holds long stalks of water plants in bill when courting (weed dance, see inset). Its legs are positioned far back on the body, making it difficult to walk on ground. Shortly after choosing a large lake for breeding, it rarely flies until late in summer. Young ride on backs of adults, climbing on minutes after hatching. Nests in large colonies of up to 100 pairs on lakes with tall vegetation.

soaring

juvenile

soaring
juvenile

Bald Eagle

Haliaeetus leucocephalus

YEAR-ROUND
WINTER

Size: 31–37" (79–94 cm); up to 7½' wingspan

Male: White head and tail contrast sharply with the dark-brown-to-black body and wings. Large, curved yellow bill and yellow feet.

Female: same as male but larger

Juvenile: dark brown with white speckles and spots on the body and wings; gray bill

Nest: massive platform, usually in a tree; female and male build; 1 brood per year

Eggs: 2–3; off-white without markings

Incubation: 34–36 days; female and male incubate

Fledging: 75–90 days; female and male feed the young

Migration: complete migrator to partial, to the Southwest; non-migrator in parts of Nevada

Food: fish, carrion, birds (mainly ducks)

Compare: The Golden Eagle (p. 213) and Turkey Vulture (p. 43) lack the white head and white tail of adult Bald Eagle. The juvenile Golden Eagle, with its white wrist marks and white base of tail, is similar to the juvenile Bald Eagle.

Stan's Notes: Nearly became extinct due to DDT poisoning and illegal killing. Returns to the same nest each year, adding more sticks and enlarging it to huge proportions, at times up to 1,000 pounds (450 kg). In their midair mating ritual, one eagle flips upside down and locks talons with another. Both tumble, then break apart to continue flight. Not uncommon for juveniles to perform this mating ritual even though they have not reached breeding age. Long-term pair bond but will switch mates when not successful at reproducing. Juveniles attain the white head and tail at 4–5 years of age.

SUMMER

Blue-gray Gnatcatcher
Polioptila caerulea

Size: 4" (10 cm)

Male: A light-blue-to-gray head, back, breast, and wings, with a white belly. Black forehead and eyebrows. Prominent white eye-ring. Long black tail with a white undertail, often held cocked above the rest of body.

Female: same as male but grayer and lacking black on the head

Juvenile: similar to female

Nest: cup; female and male construct; 1–2 broods per year

Eggs: 4–5; pale blue with dark markings

Incubation: 10–13 days; female and male incubate

Fledging: 10–12 days; female and male feed the young

Migration: complete, to Mexico and Central America

Food: insects

Compare: The only small blue bird with a black tail. Very active near the nest, look for it flitting around upper branches in search of insects.

Stan's Notes: Found in a wide variety of forest types throughout Nevada. Has been increasing and expanding its range northward along the eastern slope of the Rockies over the past few decades. Listen for its wheezy call notes to help locate it. A fun and easy bird to watch. Flicks its tail up and down and from side to side while calling. Like many open-woodland nesters, it is a common cowbird host. Returns to Nevada by mid-April, with most leaving by the end of August.

female
p. 105

male

Lazuli Bunting
Passerina amoena

SUMMER MIGRATION

Size: 5½" (14 cm)

Male: A turquoise-blue head, neck, back, and tail. Cinnamon chest with cinnamon extending down flanks slightly. White belly. Two bold white wing bars. Non-breeding male has a spotty blue head and back.

Female: overall grayish brown, warm-brown breast, a light wash of blue on wings and tail, gray throat, light-gray belly, and 2 narrow white wing bars

Juvenile: similar to adult of the same sex

Nest: cup; female builds; 2–3 broods per year

Eggs: 3–5; pale blue without markings

Incubation: 11–13 days; female incubates

Fledging: 10–12 days; female and male feed young

Migration: complete, to Mexico

Food: insects, seeds

Compare: The Western Bluebird (p. 79) is larger, darker blue, has a darker-brown breast, and lacks white wing bars.

Stan's Notes: Most common in shrublands throughout the state. Doesn't like dense forests. Strong association with water such as rivers and streams. Gathers in small flocks and tends to move up in elevations after breeding to hunt for insects and look for seeds. Has increased in population and expanded its range over the last century. Males sing from short shrubs and scrubby areas to attract females. Rarely perches on tall trees. Each male has his own unique combination of notes to produce his "own" song.

Tree Swallow
Tachycineta bicolor

SUMMER
MIGRATION

Size: 5–6" (13–15 cm)

Male: Blue-green in spring, greener in fall. Changes color in direct sunlight. White from chin to belly. Long, pointed wing tips. Notched tail.

Female: similar to male but duller

Juvenile: gray-brown with a white belly and a grayish breast band

Nest: cavity; female and male line a vacant woodpecker cavity or nest box; 2 broods per year

Eggs: 4–6; white without markings

Incubation: 13–16 days; female incubates

Fledging: 20–24 days; female and male feed the young

Migration: complete, to Mexico and Central America

Food: insects

Compare: The Barn Swallow (p. 77) has a rusty belly and a long, deeply forked tail. Similar size as the Cliff Swallow (p. 107) and Violet-green Swallow (p. 291), but it lacks any tan-to-rust color of the Cliff Swallow and any emerald green of the Violet-green Swallow.

Stan's Notes: The first swallow species to return each spring. Most common along ponds, lakes, and agricultural fields. Can be attracted to your yard with a nest box. Competes with Western and Mountain Bluebirds for cavities and nest boxes. Builds a grass nest within and will travel long distances, looking for dropped feathers for the lining. Watch for it playing and chasing after feathers. Flies with rapid wingbeats, then glides. Gives a series of gurgles and chirps. Chatters when upset or threatened. Eats many nuisance bugs. Gathers in large flocks to migrate.

Barn Swallow

Hirundo rustica

SUMMER
MIGRATION

Size:	7" (18 cm)
Male:	Sleek swallow. Blue-black back, cinnamon belly, and reddish-brown chin. White spots on a long, deeply forked tail.
Female:	same as male but with a whitish belly
Juvenile:	similar to adults, with a tan belly and chin, and shorter tail
Nest:	cup; female and male build; 2 broods per year
Eggs:	4–5; white with brown markings
Incubation:	13–17 days; female and male incubate
Fledging:	18–23 days; female and male feed the young
Migration:	complete, to South America
Food:	insects (prefers beetles, wasps, flies)
Compare:	Tree Swallow (p. 75) has a white belly and chin and a notched tail. Cliff Swallow (p. 107) and Violet-green Swallow (p. 291) are smaller and lack a distinctive, deeply forked tail. Violet-green Swallow is green with a white face. Look for Barn Swallow's deeply forked tail.

Stan's Notes: Seen in wetlands, farms, suburban yards, and parks. Of the seven swallow species regularly found in Nevada, this is the only one with a deeply forked tail. Unlike other swallows, it rarely glides in flight. Usually flies low over land or water. Drinks as it flies, skimming water, or will sip water droplets on wet leaves. Bathes while flying through rain or sprinklers. Gives a twittering warble, followed by a mechanical sound. Builds a mud nest with up to 1,000 beak-loads of mud. Nests on barns and houses, under bridges and in other sheltered places. Often nests in colonies of 4–6 birds; sometimes nests alone.

Western Bluebird
Sialia mexicana

SUMMER
WINTER

Size: 7" (18 cm)

Male: Deep blue head, neck, throat, back, wings, and tail. Rusty-red chest and flanks.

Female: similar to male, only duller with a gray head

Juvenile: similar to female, with a speckled chest

Nest: cavity, old woodpecker cavity, wooden nest box; female builds; 1–2 broods per year

Eggs: 4–6; pale blue without markings

Incubation: 13–14 days; female incubates

Fledging: 22–23 days; female and male feed young

Migration: complete, to southwestern states and Mexico

Food: insects, fruit

Compare: The Mountain Bluebird (p. 81) is similar but lacks the rusty-red breast. Male Lazuli Bunting (p. 73) is smaller and has white wing bars.

Stan's Notes: Not as common and widespread as the Mountain Bluebird. Found in a variety of habitats, from agricultural land to clear-cuts. Requires a cavity for nesting. Competes with starlings for nest cavities. Like the Mountain Bluebird, it uses nest boxes, which are responsible for the stable populations. A courting male will fly in front of the female, spread his wings and tail, and perch next to her. Often goes in and out of its nest box or cavity as if to say, "Look inside." Male may offer food to the female to establish a pair bond.

Mountain Bluebird
Sialia currucoides

YEAR-ROUND
SUMMER
WINTER

Size: 7" (18 cm)

Male: Overall sky-blue bird with a darker blue head, back, wings, and tail. White lower belly. Thin black bill.

Female: similar to male, but paler with a nearly gray head and chest and a whitish belly

Juvenile: similar to adult of the same sex

Nest: cavity, old woodpecker cavity, wooden nest box; female builds; 1–2 broods per year

Eggs: 4–6; pale blue without markings

Incubation: 13–14 days; female incubates

Fledging: 22–23 days; female and male feed young

Migration: complete, to southwestern states and Mexico; non-migrator in southern Nevada

Food: insects, fruit

Compare: Western Bluebird (p. 79) is similar, but it is darker blue with a rusty-red chest.

Stan's Notes: Common in open mountainous country, this bird nests throughout Nevada. Main diet is insects. Often hovers just before diving to the ground to grab an insect. Due to conservation of suitable nesting sites (dead trees with cavities and man-made nest boxes), populations have increased over the past 40 years. Like other bluebirds, Mountain Bluebirds take well to nest boxes and tolerate close contact with people. Female sits on baby birds (brood) for up to six days after the eggs hatch. Young imprint on their first nest box or cavity and then choose a similar type of box or cavity throughout their life. Any open field is a good place to look for Mountain Bluebirds.

Woodhouse's Scrub-Jay
Aphelocoma woodhouseii

YEAR-ROUND

Size: 11" (28 cm)

Male: Blue head, wings, tail, and breast band. Brownish patch on back. Dull white chin, breast, and belly. Very long tail.

Female: same as male

Juvenile: similar to adult, overall gray with light-blue wings and tail

Nest: cup; female and male construct; 1 brood per year

Eggs: 3–6; pale green with red-brown markings

Incubation: 15–17 days; female incubates

Fledging: 18–20 days; female and male feed young

Migration: non-migrator; moves around to find food in winter

Food: insects, seeds, fruit; comes to seed feeders

Compare: Same size as the Pinyon Jay (p. 85), which lacks the white chest and belly. Same size as the Steller's Jay (p. 87), but lacks the black head and pointed crest.

Stan's Notes: A tame bird of urban areas that visits feeders. Forms a long-term pair bond, with the male feeding female before and during incubation. Young of a pair remain close by for up to a couple years, helping parents raise subsequent brothers and sisters. Caches food by burying it for later consumption. Likely serves as a major distributor of oaks and pines by not returning to eat the seeds it buried.

Pinyon Jay

Gymnorhinus cyanocephalus

YEAR-ROUND

Size: 11" (28 cm)

Male: A short-tailed dull-blue jay. Head is darker blue than rest of body. Faint white streaks on chin. Long, pointed black bill. Black legs.

Female: same as male

Juvenile: overall gray with blue highlights

Nest: cup; female and male construct; 1 brood per year

Eggs: 4–5; blue, green, gray, or white with brown markings

Incubation: 16–17 days; female incubates

Fledging: 19–21 days; female and male feed young

Migration: non-migrator; moves around to find food

Food: seeds, insects, fruit

Compare: The Woodhouse's Scrub-Jay (p. 83) has a white chest and belly. Steller's Jay (p. 87) has a black head and crest.

Stan's Notes: Highly specialized jay, usually seen near piñon pine trees. Gathers nuts from piñon cones, storing them in large caches often on the ground. An important seed disperser, with forgotten caches sprouting into new trees. Can breed in late winter in years with abundant seed production. Gregarious, it breeds in colonies of up to 50 pairs. Starts breeding at age 3. Mates often the same age stay together for years. In winter flocks of up to several hundred gather to roost and find food, and move on when supplies are low. Has a soft flight song of, "hoyi-hoyi-hoyi-hoyi." Often walks rather than hops, like most other jays. Closely related to Clark's Nutcracker.

Steller's Jay
Cyanocitta stelleri

YEAR-ROUND

Size: 11" (28 cm)

Male: Dark-blue wings, tail, and belly. Black head, nape of the neck, and chest. Large, pointed black crest on head that can be lifted at will. Distinctive white streaks on forehead and just above eyes.

Female: same as male

Juvenile: similar to adult

Nest: cup; female and male construct; 1 brood per year

Eggs: 3–5; pale bluish green with brown markings

Incubation: 14–16 days; female incubates

Fledging: 16–18 days; female and male feed the young

Migration: non-migrator; moves around to find food

Food: insects, berries, seeds; will visit seed feeders

Compare: The Woodhouse's Scrub-Jay (p. 83) and Pinyon Jay (p. 85) are the same size, but lack the black head and crest of the Steller's Jay.

Stan's Notes: Common resident of foothills and lower mountains from 6,000 to 8,000 feet (1,850–2,450 m). Usually only found in conifer forests. Thought to mate for life, rarely dispersing far, usually breeding within 10 miles (16 km) of the place of birth. Several subspecies found throughout the Rockies. Nevada form has a black crest with distinct white streaks, while others lack white markings. Named after the Arctic explorer Georg W. Steller, who is said to have first recorded the bird on the coast of Alaska in 1741.

male

female

Belted Kingfisher
Megaceryle alcyon

YEAR-ROUND
WINTER

Size: 12–14" (30–36 cm)

Male: Blue with white belly, blue-gray chest band, and black wing tips. Ragged crest moves up and down at will. Large head. Long, thick, black bill. White spot by eyes. Red-brown eyes.

Female: same as male but with rusty flanks and a rusty chest band below the blue-gray band

Juvenile: similar to female

Nest: cavity; female and male excavate in a bank of a river, lake, or cliff; 1 brood per year

Eggs: 6–7; white without markings

Incubation: 23–24 days; female and male incubate

Fledging: 27–29 days; female and male feed the young

Migration: non-migrator to partial migrator in Nevada

Food: small fish

Compare: The Woodhouse's Scrub-Jay (p. 83) is smaller. The Belted Kingfisher is rarely found away from water.

Stan's Notes: Usually found at the bank of a river, lake, or large stream. Perches on a branch near water, dives in headfirst to catch a small fish, then returns to the branch to feed. Parents drop dead fish into the water to teach their young to dive. Can't pass bones through its digestive tract; regurgitates bone pellets after meals. Loud call that sounds like a machine gun. Mates know each other by their calls. Digs a tunnel up to 4 feet (about 1 m) long to a nest chamber. Small white patches on dark wing tips flash during flight. Many northern birds move into Nevada in winter, increasing the population.

Brown Creeper
Certhia americana

YEAR-ROUND
WINTER

Size: 5" (13 cm)

Male: Small, thin, nearly camouflaged brown bird. White from chin to belly. White eyebrows. Dark eyes and a thin, curved bill. Tail is long and stiff.

Female: same as male

Juvenile: same as adults

Nest: cup; female constructs; 1 brood per year

Eggs: 5–6; white with tiny brown markings

Incubation: 14–17 days; female incubates; male feeds the female during incubation

Fledging: 13–16 days; female and male feed the young

Migration: partial migrator to non-migrator; moves around in winter to find food

Food: insects, nuts, seeds

Compare: The Red-breasted Nuthatch (p. 221) and White-breasted Nuthatch (p. 233) climb down tree trunks, not up. To spot a Brown Creeper, look for a small brown bird with a white belly creeping up trees.

Stan's Notes: A forest bird, commonly found in wooded habitats. Will fly from the top of one tree trunk to the bottom of another, then work its way to the top, looking for caterpillars, spider eggs, and more. Its long tail has tiny spines underneath, which help it cling to trees. Uses its camouflage coloring to hide in plain sight: it spreads out flat on a branch or trunk and won't move. Often builds its nest behind the loose bark of a dead or dying tree. Young follow their parents around, creeping up trees soon after fledging.

Chipping Sparrow
Spizella passerina

SUMMER

Size: 5" (13 cm)

Male: Small gray-brown sparrow with clear-gray chest. Rusty crown. White eyebrows and thin black eye line. Thin gray-black bill. Two faint wing bars.

Female: same as male

Juvenile: similar to adults, with streaking on the chest; lacks a rusty crown

Nest: cup; female builds; 2 broods per year

Eggs: 3–5; blue-green with brown markings

Incubation: 11–14 days; female incubates

Fledging: 10–12 days; female and male feed the young

Migration: complete to Arizona, New Mexico, Mexico, and Central America

Food: insects, seeds; will come to ground feeders

Compare: The Lark Sparrow (p. 121) is larger and has a white chest and central spot. Song Sparrow (p. 101) and female House Finch (p. 97) have heavily streaked chests.

Stan's Notes: A common garden or yard bird, often seen feeding on dropped seeds beneath feeders. Gathers in large family groups to feed in preparation for migration. Migrates at night in flocks of 20–30 birds. The common name comes from the male's fast "chip" call. Often is just called Chippy. Builds nest low in dense shrubs and almost always lines it with animal hair. Comfortable with people, allowing you to approach closely before it flies away.

Pine Siskin
Spinus pinus

YEAR-ROUND
WINTER

Size: 5" (13 cm)

Male: Small brown finch with heavy streaking on the back, breast, and belly. Yellow wing bars. Yellow at the base of tail. Thin bill.

Female: similar to male, with less yellow

Juvenile: similar to adult, with a light-yellow tinge over the breast and chin

Nest: cup; female builds; 2 broods

Eggs: 3–4; greenish blue with brown markings

Incubation: 12–13 days; female incubates

Fledging: 14–15 days; female and male feed the young

Migration: irruptive; moves around the state in search of food in winter

Food: seeds, insects; will come to seed feeders

Compare: Female House Finch (p. 97) lacks any yellow. The female American Goldfinch (p. 325) has white wing bars. Look for the yellow wing bars to identify the Pine Siskin.

Stan's Notes: A nesting resident, it is usually considered a winter finch because it is more visible in the non-nesting season, when it gathers in flocks, moves around the state, and visits bird feeders. Seen in flocks of up to 20 birds, often with other finch species. Will come to thistle feeders. Gives a series of high-pitched, wheezy calls. Also gives a wheezing twitter. Breeds in small groups. Builds nest toward the end of coniferous branches, where needles are dense, helping to conceal. Nests are often only a few feet apart. Male feeds the female during incubation. Juveniles lose the yellow tint by late summer of their first year.

male
p. 307

female

House Wren

Troglodytes aedon

YEAR-ROUND
SUMMER
WINTER

Size: 5" (13 cm)

Male: All-brown bird with lighter-brown markings on the wings and tail. Slightly curved brown bill. Often holds tail upward.

Female: same as male

Juvenile: same as adult

Nest: cavity; female and male line just about any nest cavity; 2 broods per year

Eggs: 4–6; cream with brown markings

Incubation: 10–13 days; female incubates

Fledging: 12–15 days; female and male feed the young

Migration: complete, to Arizona, New Mexico, Mexico

Food: insects, spiders, snails

Compare: The Canyon Wren (p. 111), Rock Wren (p. 113), and Bewick's Wren (p. 109) are slightly larger. Canyon Wren has a distinctive white throat and chest and a long down-curved bill. Rock Wren has fine white speckles on the back with a light-tan belly and chest. The Bewick's Wren has white eyebrows.

Stan's Notes: A prolific songster. During the mating season, sings from dawn to dusk. Seen in brushy yards, parks, and woodlands and along forest edges. Easily attracted to a nest box. In spring, the male chooses several prospective nesting cavities and places a few small twigs in each. The female inspects all of them and finishes constructing the nest in the cavity of her choice. She fills the cavity with short twigs and then lines a small depression at the back with pine needles and grass. She often has trouble fitting longer twigs through the entrance hole and tries many different directions and approaches until she is successful.

Song Sparrow

Melospiza melodia

YEAR-ROUND

Size: 5–6" (13–15 cm)

Male: Common brown sparrow with heavy dark streaks on the chest coalescing into a central dark spot.

Female: same as male

Juvenile: similar to adults, with a finely streaked chest; lacks a central dark spot

Nest: cup; female builds; 2 broods per year

Eggs: 3–4; blue to green, with red-brown markings

Incubation: 12–14 days; female incubates

Fledging: 9–12 days; female and male feed the young

Migration: non-migrator in Nevada

Food: insects, seeds; only rarely comes to ground feeders with seeds

Compare: Similar to other brown sparrows. Look for the heavily streaked chest with a central dark spot to help identify the Song Sparrow.

Stan's Notes: There are many subspecies of this bird, but the dark spot in the center of the chest appears in every variety. A constant songster, repeating its loud, clear song every few minutes. The song varies from region to region but has the same basic structure. Sings from thick shrubs to defend a small territory, beginning with three notes and finishing up with a trill. A ground feeder, it will "double-scratch" with both feet at the same time to expose seeds. When the female builds a new nest for a second brood, the male often takes over feeding the first brood. Unlike many other sparrow species, Song Sparrows rarely flock together. A common host of the Brown-headed Cowbird.

male
p. 231

female

gray-headed

Oregon
female

Dark-eyed Junco
Junco hyemalis

YEAR-ROUND
WINTER

Size: 5½" (14 cm)

Female: A plump, dark-eyed bird with a tan-to-brown chest, head, and back. White belly. Ivory-to-pink bill. White outer tail feathers appear like a white V in flight.

Male: round bird with gray plumage

Juvenile: similar to female, with streaking on the breast and head

Nest: cup on the ground; female builds; 2 broods per year

Eggs: 3–5; white with reddish-brown markings

Incubation: 12–13 days; female incubates

Fledging: 10–13 days; male and female feed the young

Migration: partial migrator to non-migrator in Nevada

Food: seeds, insects; visits ground and seed feeders

Compare: Rarely confused with any other bird. Look for the ivory-to-pink bill and small flocks feeding beneath seed feeders to help identify the female Dark-eyed Junco.

Stan's Notes: One of the most numerous birds in the state. Common year-round bird of Nevada, spending winters in foothills and plains after snowmelt, returning to higher elevations for nesting. Adheres to a rigid social hierarchy, with dominant birds chasing the less dominant birds. Look for the white outer tail feathers flashing in flight. Often seen in small flocks on the ground, where it uses its feet to simultaneously "double-scratch" to expose seeds and insects. Eats many weed seeds. Nests in a wide variety of wooded habitats in April and May. Several subspecies of Dark-eyed Junco were previously considered to be separate species (see lower insets).

female

male
p. 73

Lazuli Bunting
Passerina amoena

SUMMER
MIGRATION

Size: 5½" (14 cm)

Female: Overall grayish brown with a warm brown chest, light wash of blue on wings and tail, gray throat, and light-gray belly. Two narrow white wing bars.

Male: turquoise-blue head, neck, back, and tail; cinnamon breast, white belly, 2 bold white wing bars

Juvenile: similar to adult of the same sex

Nest: cup; female builds; 2–3 broods per year

Eggs: 3–5; pale blue without markings

Incubation: 11–13 days; female incubates

Fledging: 10–12 days; female and male feed the young

Migration: complete, to Mexico

Food: insects, seeds

Compare: Female Western (p. 79) and Mountain Bluebirds (p. 81) are larger and have much more blue than female Bunting.

Stan's Notes: More common in shrublands throughout the state. Doesn't like dense forests. Strong association with water such as rivers and streams. Gathers in small flocks and tends to move up in elevations after breeding to hunt for insects and look for seeds. Has increased in population and expanded its range over the last century. Males sing from short shrubs and scrubby areas to attract females. Rarely perches on tall trees. Each male has his own unique combination of notes to produce his "own" song.

Cliff Swallow

Petrochelidon pyrrhonota

SUMMER MIGRATION

Size: 5½" (14 cm)

Male: Uniquely patterned swallow with a dark back, wings, and cap. Distinctive tan-to-rust rump, cheeks, and forehead.

Female: same as male

Juvenile: similar to adult, lacks distinct patterning

Nest: gourd-shaped, made of mud; male and female build; 1–2 broods per year

Eggs: 4–6; white with brown markings

Incubation: 14–16 days; male and female incubate

Fledging: 21–24 days; female and male feed young

Migration: complete, to South America

Food: insects

Compare: Barn Swallow (p. 77) is larger and has a distinctive, deeply forked tail and blue back and wings. Tree Swallow (p. 75) lacks any tan-to-rust coloring. Violet-green Swallow (p. 291) is green with a bright-white face.

Stan's Notes: A common and widespread swallow species in Nevada during summer. Common around bridges (especially bridges over water) and rural housing (especially in open country near cliffs). Builds a gourd-shaped nest with a funnel-like entrance pointing down. A colony nester, with many nests lined up beneath building eaves or cliff overhangs. Will carry balls of mud up to a mile to construct its nest. Many in the colony return to the same nest site each year. Not unusual to have two broods per season. If the number of nests underneath eaves becomes a problem, wait until the young have left the nests to hose off the mud.

Eastern

Western

Bewick's Wren
Thryomanes bewickii

Size: 5½" (14 cm)

Male: Brown cap, back, wings, and tail. Gray chest and belly. White chin and eyebrows. Long tail with white spots on edges is cocked and flits sideways. Pointed down-curved bill.

Female: same as male

Juvenile: similar to adult

Nest: cavity; female and male build nest in woodpecker hole or nest box; 2–3 broods a year

Eggs: 4–8; white with brown markings

Incubation: 12–14 days; female incubates

Fledging: 10–14 days; female and male feed young

Migration: non-migrator; moves around in winter to find food

Food: insects, seeds

Compare: The House Wren (p. 99) is slightly smaller and lacks the obvious white eyebrow marks and white spots on tail. The Rock Wren (p. 113) has a gray back with white spots.

Stan's Notes: A common wren of backyards and gardens. Insects make up 97 percent of its diet, with plant seeds composing the rest. Competes with House Wrens for nesting cavities. Male will choose nesting cavities and start to build nests using small uniform-sized sticks. Female will make the final selection of a nest site and finish building. Begins breeding in April and has as 2–3 broods per year. Male feeds female while she incubates. Average size territory per pair is 5 acres (2 ha), which they defend all year long.

Canyon Wren
Catherpes mexicanus

YEAR-ROUND

Size: 5¾" (14.5 cm)

Male: Chestnut back, wings, belly, and tail. Gray head and nape of neck. A distinctive white throat and chest. Long downward-curving bill. Tail often cocked up.

Female: same as male

Juvenile: similar to adult

Nest: crevice; male and female build; 1–2 broods per year

Eggs: 4–6; white with light-brown markings

Incubation: 14–16 days; female and male incubate

Fledging: 14–18 days; female and male feed young

Migration: non-migrator to partial; moves around to find food

Food: insects

Compare: Rock Wren (p. 113) is slightly larger and tends to be more grayish, with white chin not as prominent. House Wren (p. 99) is slightly smaller and lacks the large bill of the Canyon Wren.

Stan's Notes: An active wren, spending its entire life among rocks and cliffs. Prefers steep-sided canyons, hence its common name. Maintains winter territories, usually around running water, to hunt for winter-active insects. Territories are up to 2 acres (1 ha) in size. Nests are attached to rocks within crevices that usually have some kind of rock covering. May reuse the nest from year to year. Lives in close association with Rock Wrens, which use scattered boulders and rocks for nesting.

Rock Wren
Salpinctes obsoletus

YEAR-ROUND SUMMER

Size: 6" (15 cm)

Male: Overall grayish brown with tinges of buffy brown on tail and wings. Gray back, often finely speckled with white. Belly and breast are light tan.

Female: same as male

Juvenile: similar to adult

Nest: crevice; male and female build; 2–3 broods per year

Eggs: 4–8; white with light-brown markings

Incubation: 14–16 days; female incubates

Fledging: 14–18 days; female and male feed young

Migration: complete migrator, to southwestern states; non-migrator in southern half of Nevada

Food: insects

Compare: Canyon Wren (p. 111) is slightly smaller, mostly chestnut brown, and has a much larger and down-curved bill. House Wren (p. 99) is slightly smaller and lacks Rock Wren's white speckles on back.

Stan's Notes: Consistently uses open sunny piles of broken rocks (scree) and rock debris at cliff bases (talus slopes) for nesting. Often builds a small runway of flat stones leading up to the nest, which is usually in a rock crevice. Known to also nest on prairies, where it uses dirt banks instead of rock piles. Begins nesting in May, with the female doing most of the incubating and the male feeding the female during incubation. Lives in close association with Canyon Wrens, which use steep-sided canyons for nesting.

male

female

House Sparrow

Passer domesticus

YEAR-ROUND

Size: 6" (15 cm)

Male: Brown back with a gray belly and cap. Large black patch extending from the throat to the chest (bib). One white wing bar.

Female: slightly smaller than the male; light brown with light eyebrows; lacks a bib and white wing bar

Juvenile: similar to female

Nest: cavity; female and male build a domed cup nest within; 2–3 broods per year

Eggs: 4–6; white with brown markings

Incubation: 10–12 days; female and male incubate

Fledging: 14–17 days; female and male feed the young

Migration: non-migrator; moves around to find food

Food: seeds, insects, fruit; comes to seed feeders

Compare: Chipping Sparrow (p. 93) has a rusty-red crown. Look for the black bib to identify the male House Sparrow and the clear breast to help identify the female.

Stan's Notes: One of the first birdsongs heard in cities in spring. A familiar city bird, nearly always in small flocks. Also found on farms. Introduced in 1851 from Europe to Central Park in New York. Now seen throughout North America. Related to old-world sparrows; not a relative of any sparrows in the US. An aggressive bird that will kill young birds in order to take over the nest cavity. Uses dried grass and small scraps of plastic, paper, and other materials to build an oversize, domed nest in the cavity.

male

female

Gray-crowned Rosy-Finch
Leucosticte tephrocotis

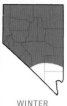

WINTER

Size: 6" (15 cm)

Male: Gray crown with a black forehead, chin, and throat. Warm cinnamon-brown body with a wash of rosy red, especially along flanks and rump.

Female: same as male, but has less red

Juvenile: similar to adult of the same sex

Nest: cup; female builds; 1–2 broods per year

Eggs: 3–5; white without markings

Incubation: 12–14 days; female incubates

Fledging: 16–18 days; female and male feed young

Migration: complete migrator, to higher elevations of western states; winters in Nevada

Food: seeds, insects; will visit seed feeders

Compare: The female Cassin's Finch (p. 121) and female House Finch (p. 97) lack the characteristic gray crown of Gray-crowned Rosy-Finch.

Stan's Notes: Found in high alpine regions. Breeds in the Rocky Mountains of Canada and the US and moves into Nevada in winter. Almost always seen in small flocks, foraging on the ground near patches of snow in high elevations. Nests in steep cliff faces. During breeding, both male and female develop an opening in the floor of the mouth (buccal pouch), which is used to carry a large supply of food, such as insects, to young in the nest.

male
p. 309

female

Cassin's Finch
Haemorhous cassinii

YEAR-ROUND
WINTER

Size: 6½" (16 cm)

Female: Brown-to-gray finch with fine black streaks on back and wings. Heavily streaked white chest and belly.

Male: light wash of crimson red, especially bright-red crown, brown streaks on the back and wings, white belly

Juvenile: similar to female

Nest: cup; female builds; 1–2 broods per year

Eggs: 3–5; bluish green with brown markings

Incubation: 12–14 days; female incubates

Fledging: 14–18 days; female and male feed young

Migration: partial migrator to non-migrator; will move around to find food

Food: seeds, insects, fruits, berries; will visit seed feeders

Compare: The female House Finch (p. 97) is similar, but it has a gray belly that is not as streaked. Lacks the characteristic gray head markings of the Gray-crowned Rosy-Finch (p. 117).

Stan's Notes: This is a mountain finch of coniferous forests. Usually forages for seeds on the ground, but it also eats evergreen buds and aspen and willow catkins. A colony nester, depending on the regional source of food. The more food available, the larger the colony. Male sings a rapid warble, often imitating other birds, such as jays, tanagers, and grosbeaks. A cowbird host.

Lark Sparrow
Chondestes grammacus

Size: 6½" (16 cm)

Male: All-brown bird with unique rust-red, white, and black head pattern. A white breast with a central black spot. Gray rump and white edges to gray tail, as seen in flight.

Female: same as male

Juvenile: similar to adult, but no rust-red on head

Nest: cup, on the ground; female builds; 1–2 broods per year

Eggs: 3–6; pale white with brown markings

Incubation: 10–12 days; female incubates

Fledging: 10–12 days; female and male feed young

Migration: complete, to coastal Mexico

Food: seeds, insects

Compare: The White-crowned Sparrow (p. 123) lacks the Lark Sparrow's rust-red pattern on the head and central spot on a white chest. Larger than the Chipping Sparrow (p. 93), which has a similar rusty color on head but lacks Lark Sparrow's white breast and central spot.

Stan's Notes: One of the larger sparrow species and one of the best songsters, also well known for its courtship strutting, chasing, and lark-like flight pattern (rapid wingbeats with tail spread). A bird of open fields, pastures and prairies, found almost anywhere. Very common during migration, when large flocks congregate. Will use nest for several years if first brood is successful.

juvenile

White-crowned Sparrow
Zonotrichia leucophrys

YEAR-ROUND
WINTER

Size: 6½–7½" (16.5–19 cm)

Male: Brown with a gray chest and black-and-white striped crown. Small, thin, pink or yellow bill.

Female: same as male

Juvenile: similar to adults, with black and brown stripes on the head

Nest: cup; female builds; 2 broods per year

Eggs: 3–5; greenish to bluish to whitish with red-brown markings

Incubation: 11–14 days; female incubates

Fledging: 8–12 days; male and female feed the young

Migration: complete migrator, to southwestern states and Mexico; non-migrator in parts of Nevada

Food: insects, seeds, berries; visits ground feeders

Compare: The Lark Sparrow (p. 121) has a rust-red pattern on the head and a central black spot on a white breast.

Stan's Notes: Year-round resident in the northern half of Nevada and a winter visitor in the southern half. Often in groups of up to 20 birds during migration, when it can be seen feeding underneath seed feeders. This ground feeder will "double-scratch" backward with both feet simultaneously to find seeds. Nesting begins in April and May. The males are prolific songsters, singing in late winter while migrating north. Males arrive at the breeding grounds before the females and sing from perches to establish territory. Males take most of the responsibility for raising the young while females start their second broods. Only 9–12 days separate the broods.

Fox Sparrow
Passerella iliaca

SUMMER MIGRATION

Size:	7" (18 cm)
Male:	A plump, brown sparrow with a gray head, back and rump. White chest and belly with rusty brown streaks. Rusty tail and wings.
Female:	same as male
Juvenile:	same as adult
Nest:	cup; female builds; 1 brood per year
Eggs:	2–4; pale green with reddish markings
Incubation:	12–14 days; female incubates
Fledging:	10–11 days; male and female feed the young
Migration:	complete to coastal California, Arizona, and New Mexico
Food:	seeds, insects; comes to ground feeders
Compare:	The Spotted Towhee (p. 27) is found in similar habitats, but the male towhee has a black head and both male and female have white bellies.

Stan's Notes: One of the largest sparrows. Often alone or in small groups. Found in shrubby areas, open fields, and backyards. Comes to ground feeders and often seen underneath seed feeders during migration, searching for seeds and insects. Like a chicken, it will "double-scratch" with both feet at the same time to look for food. Gives a series of rich notes lasting 2–3 seconds, usually singing from a perch hidden in a shrub. The common name "Sparrow" comes from the Anglo-Saxon word *spearwa*, meaning "flutterer," and applies to any small bird. "Fox" refers to its rusty color. Appears in several color variations, depending on the part of the country. Fox Sparrows in western states have gray heads and backs.

female

male

Horned Lark
Eremophila alpestris

YEAR-ROUND

Size: 7–8" (18–20 cm)

Male: Tan to brown with black markings on the face. Black necklace and bill. Pale-yellow chin. Two tiny feather "horns" on the top of the head, sometimes hard to see. Dark tail with white outer tail feathers, seen in flight.

Female: duller than male; less noticeable "horns"

Juvenile: lacks a yellow chin and black markings; does not develop "horns" until the second year

Nest: ground; female builds; 2–3 broods per year

Eggs: 3–4; gray with brown markings

Incubation: 11–12 days; female incubates

Fledging: 9–12 days; female and male feed the young

Migration: non-migrator; moves around to find food in winter

Food: seeds, insects

Compare: Western Meadowlark (p. 345) is larger and has a yellow breast and belly. Look for the black markings by the eyes and the black necklace to identify the Horned Lark.

Stan's Notes: The only true lark native to North America. A bird of open ground. Common in rural areas; often seen in large flocks. The population increased in North America over the past century as more land was cleared for farming. Male performs a fluttering courtship flight high in the air while singing a high-pitched song. Female performs a fluttering distraction display when the nest is disturbed. Starts breeding early in the year. Able to renest about a week after the brood fledges. Moves around in winter to find food. "Lark" comes from the Middle English *laverock*, or "a lark."

female

Brown-headed Cowbird
Molothrus ater

YEAR-ROUND
SUMMER

Size:	7½" (19 cm)
Female:	Dull brown with no obvious markings. Pointed, sharp, gray bill. Dark eyes.
Male:	glossy black with a chocolate-brown head
Juvenile:	similar to female but with dull-gray plumage and a streaked chest
Nest:	no nest; lays eggs in the nests of other birds
Eggs:	5–7; white with brown markings
Incubation:	10–13 days; host birds incubate the eggs
Fledging:	10–11 days; host birds feed the young
Migration:	complete, to Arizona and New Mexico; non-migrator in parts of the state
Food:	insects, seeds; will come to seed feeders
Compare:	The female Red-winged Blackbird (p. 137) has white eyebrows and heavy streaking. The pointed gray bill helps to identify the female Brown-headed Cowbird.

Stan's Notes: Cowbirds are members of the blackbird family. Of approximately 750 species of parasitic birds worldwide, this is the only parasitic bird in Nevada. Brood parasites lay their eggs in the nests of other birds, leaving the host birds to raise their young. Cowbirds are known to have laid their eggs in the nests of over 200 species of birds. While some birds reject cowbird eggs, most incubate them and raise the young, even to the exclusion of their own. Look for warblers and other birds feeding young birds twice their own size. Named "Cowbird" for its habit of following bison and cattle herds to feed on insects flushed up by the animals.

1 year old

Bohemian Waxwing

Cedar Waxwing
Bombycilla cedrorum

YEAR-ROUND
WINTER

Size: 7½" (19 cm)

Male: Sleek-looking, gray-to-brown bird. Pointed crest, bandit-like mask, and light-yellow belly. Bold-yellow tip of tail. Red wing tips look like they were dipped in red wax.

Female: same as male

Juvenile: grayish with a heavily streaked breast; lacks the sleek look, black mask, and red wing tips

Nest: cup; female and male construct; 1 brood per year, occasionally 2

Eggs: 4–6; pale blue with brown markings

Incubation: 10–12 days; female incubates

Fledging: 14–18 days; female and male feed the young

Migration: complete to partial migrator; moves around to find food

Food: cedar cones, fruit, insects

Compare: Similar to its larger, less common cousin, Bohemian Waxwing (see inset). Look for the red wing tips, yellow-tipped tail and black mask to identify the Cedar Waxwing.

Stan's Notes: The name is derived from its red, wax-like wing tips and preference for the small, berry-like cones of the cedar. Seen in flocks, moving around from area to area looking for berries. Feeds on insects during summer, before berries are abundant. Wanders during winter, searching for food supplies. Spends most of its time at the top of tall trees. Listen for the high-pitched "sreee" whistling sound it constantly makes while perched or in flight. Obtains the mask after the first year and red wing tips after the second year.

winter

breeding

Spotted Sandpiper

Actitis macularius

SUMMER
MIGRATION
WINTER

Size: 8" (20 cm)

Male: Olive-brown back with black spots on a white chest and belly. White line over eyes. Long, dull-yellow legs. Long bill. Winter plumage lacks spots on the chest and belly.

Female: same as male

Juvenile: similar to winter plumage, with a darker bill

Nest: ground; male and female build; 2 broods per year

Eggs: 3–4; brownish with brown markings

Incubation: 20–24 days; male incubates

Fledging: 17–21 days; male feeds the young

Migration: complete migrator, to Arizona, New Mexico, Mexico, and Central and South America

Food: aquatic insects

Compare: Killdeer (p. 149) has 2 black neck bands. Look for the black spots on the chest and belly and the bobbing tail to help identify the breeding Spotted Sandpiper.

Stan's Notes: One of the few sandpipers in Nevada. Seen along the shorelines of large ponds, lakes, and rivers. One of the few shorebirds that will dive underwater when pursued. Able to fly straight up out of the water. Holds wings in a cup-like arc in flight, rarely lifting them above a horizontal plane. Walks as if delicately balanced. When standing, constantly bobs its tail. Gives a rapid series of "weet-weet-weet" calls when frightened and flying away. Female mates with multiple males and lays eggs in up to five nests. Male does all of the incubating and childcare without any help from the female.

male
p. 305

female

Black-headed Grosbeak

Pheucticus melanocephalus

SUMMER
MIGRATION

Size: 8" (20 cm)

Female: Appears like an overgrown sparrow. Overall brown with a lighter breast and belly. Large two-toned bill. Prominent white eyebrows. Yellow wing linings, as seen in flight.

Male: burnt-orange chest, neck, and rump; black head, tail, and wings with irregular-shaped white wing patches; large bill with upper bill darker than lower

Juvenile: similar to adult of the same sex

Nest: cup; female builds; 1 brood per year

Eggs: 3–4; pale green or bluish, brown markings

Incubation: 11–13 days; female and male incubate

Fledging: 11–13 days; female and male feed young

Migration: complete, to Mexico, Central America, and South America

Food: seeds, insects, fruit; comes to seed feeders

Compare: Female House Finch (p. 97) is smaller, has more streaking on the chest and the bill isn't as large. Look for female Grosbeak's unusual bicolored bill.

Stan's Notes: A cosmopolitan bird that nests in a wide variety of habitats, seeming to prefer the foothills slightly more than other places. Both the male and female sing and will aggressively defend the nest against intruders. Song is very similar to American Robin's (p. 251) and Western Tanager's (p. 335), making it hard to tell them apart by song. Males don't get adult plumage until 2 years of age. Comes to seed feeders.

male
p. 29

female

Red-winged Blackbird

Agelaius phoeniceus

YEAR-ROUND

Size: 8½" (22 cm)

Female: Heavily streaked brown body. Pointed brown bill and white eyebrows.

Male: jet black with red-and-yellow shoulder patches (epaulets) and a pointed black bill

Juvenile: same as female

Nest: cup; female builds; 2–3 broods per year

Eggs: 3–4; bluish green with brown markings

Incubation: 10–12 days; female incubates

Fledging: 11–14 days; female and male feed the young

Migration: non-migrator to partial migrator; will move around to find food in winter

Food: seeds, insects; visits seed feeders

Compare: Female Brewer's Blackbird (p. 139) and female Yellow-headed Blackbird (p. 147) are larger. Female Brown-headed Cowbird (p. 129) is smaller. All three species lack white eyebrows and heavily streaked chest of the female Red-winged Blackbird.

Stan's Notes: One of the most widespread and numerous birds in the state. Found around marshes, wetlands, lakes, and rivers. Flocks with as many as 10,000 birds have been reported. Males arrive before females and sing to defend their territory. The male repeats his call from the top of a cattail while showing off his red-and-yellow shoulder patches. The female chooses a mate and often builds her nest over shallow water in a thick stand of cattails. The male can be aggressive when defending the nest. Feeds mostly on seeds in spring and fall, and insects throughout the summer.

male
p. 31

female

Brewer's Blackbird

Euphagus cyanocephalus

YEAR-ROUND
WINTER

Size: 9" (22.5 cm)

Female: Overall grayish brown. Legs and bill nearly black. While most have dark eyes, some have bright-white or pale-yellow eyes.

Male: glossy black, shining green in direct light, head purplish, white or pale-yellow eyes

Juvenile: similar to female

Nest: cup; female builds; 1–2 broods per year

Eggs: 4–6; gray with brown markings

Incubation: 12–14 days; female incubates

Fledging: 13–14 days; female and male feed young

Migration: non-migrator to partial migrator in Nevada

Food: insects, seeds, fruit

Compare: Female Brown-headed Cowbird (p. 129) is smaller and lighter in color. Female Red-winged Blackbird (p. 137) is similar in size, but it has a heavily streaked chest and prominent white eyebrows.

Stan's Notes: Common blackbird often found in association with agricultural lands and seen in open areas such as wet pastures and mountain meadows up to 10,000 feet (3,050 m). Male and some females are easily identified by their bright, nearly white eyes. It is a common cowbird host, usually nesting in a shrub, small tree, or directly on the ground. Prefers to nest in small colonies of up to 20 pairs. Gathers in large flocks with cowbirds, Red-wingeds and other blackbirds to migrate. It is expanding its range in North America.

female

male

Common Nighthawk
Chordeiles minor

SUMMER

Size: 9" (23 cm)

Male: Camouflaged brown and white with a white chin. Distinctive white band across the wings and tail, seen only in flight.

Female: similar to male, with a tan chin; lacks a white tail band

Juvenile: similar to female

Nest: no nest; lays eggs on the ground, usually on rocks, or on rooftop; 1 brood per year

Eggs: 2; cream with lavender markings

Incubation: 19–20 days; female incubates

Fledging: 20–21 days; female and male feed the young

Migration: complete, to South America

Food: insects caught in the air

Compare: Look for the white chin, obvious white band on the wings, and characteristic flap-flap-flap-glide pattern to help identify the Common Nighthawk.

Stan's Notes: Usually only seen in flight at dusk or after sunset but not uncommon to see it sleeping on a branch during the day. A prolific insect eater and very noisy in flight, repeating a "peenting" call. Alternates slow wingbeats with bursts of quick wingbeats. In cities, prefers to nest on flat rooftops with gravel. City populations are on the decline as gravel rooftops are converted to other styles. In spring, the male performs a showy mating ritual consisting of a steep diving flight ending with a loud popping noise. One of the first birds to migrate each fall, starting in August. Often seen in large flocks.

SUMMER

Burrowing Owl
Athene cunicularia

Size: 9–10" (24 cm); up to 2' wingspan

Male: A brown owl with bold white spots and a white belly. Yellow eyes and very long legs.

Female: same as male

Juvenile: same as adult, but belly is white

Nest: cavity, former underground mammal den; female and male line den; 1 brood per year

Eggs: 6–11; white without markings

Incubation: 26–30 days; female incubates

Fledging: 25–28 days; female and male feed young

Migration: complete, to Arizona, New Mexico, Texas, Mexico, and Central America

Food: insects, mammals, lizards, birds

Compare: Great Horned Owl (p. 203) is more than twice the size of Burrowing Owl and has feather tuft "horns." Burrowing spends most of its time on the ground, unlike tree-loving Great Horned.

Stan's Notes: An owl of fields, open backyards, golf courses, and airports. Nests in large family units or in small colonies. Takes over the underground dens of mammals, occasionally widening its den by kicking dirt backward. Lines den with cow pies, horse dung, grass, and feathers. Some people have had success attracting these owls to their backyards by creating artificial dens. Often seen during the day, standing or sleeping around den entrance. Male brings food to incubating female, often moving family to a new den when young are just a few weeks old. Will bob head up and down while doing deep knee bends when agitated or threatened.

in flight

juvenile

male

female

in-flight
juvenile

American Kestrel
Falco sparverius

YEAR-ROUND

Size: 9–11" (23–28 cm); up to 2' wingspan

Male: Rust-brown back and tail. White breast with dark spots. Two vertical black lines on a white face. Blue-gray wings. Wide black band with a white edge on the tip of a rusty tail.

Female: similar to male but slightly larger, with rust-brown wings and dark bands on the tail

Juvenile: same as adult of the same sex

Nest: cavity; does not build a nest; 1 brood per year

Eggs: 4–5; white with brown markings

Incubation: 29–31 days; male and female incubate

Fledging: 30–31 days; female and male feed the young

Migration: non-migrator in Nevada; moves around to find food

Food: insects, small mammals and birds, reptiles

Compare: The Peregrine Falcon (p. 273) is much larger and has a dark "hood" marking. No other small bird of prey has a rusty back and tail.

Stan's Notes: An unusual raptor because the sexes look different (dimorphic). Due to its small size, this falcon was once called a Sparrow Hawk. Hovers near roads, then dives for prey. Watch for it to pump its tail after landing on a perch. Perches nearly upright. Eats many grasshoppers. Adapts quickly to a wooden nest box. Can be extremely vocal, giving a loud series of high-pitched calls. Ability to see ultraviolet (UV) light helps it locate mice and other prey by their urine, which glows bright yellow in UV light.

male
p. 33

female

Yellow-headed Blackbird

Xanthocephalus xanthocephalus

YEAR-ROUND
SUMMER

Size:	9–11" (23–28 cm)
Female:	Large brown bird with a dull-yellow head and chest. Slightly smaller than the male.
Male:	black bird with a lemon-yellow head, breast, and nape of neck; black mask, gray bill, and white wing patches
Juvenile:	similar to female
Nest:	cup; female builds; 1–2 broods per year
Eggs:	3–5; greenish white with brown markings
Incubation:	11–13 days; female incubates
Fledging:	9–12 days; female and male feed the young
Migration:	complete, to Arizona, New Mexico, Mexico
Food:	insects, seeds; will come to ground feeders
Compare:	Female Red-winged Blackbird (p. 137) is smaller and has white eyebrows and heavy streaking. Look for the dull-yellow head to help identify the female Yellow-headed.

Stan's Notes: Found around marshes, wetlands, and lakes. Nests in deep water, unlike its cousin, the Red-winged Blackbird, which prefers shallow water. Usually heard before seen. Gives a raspy, low, metallic-sounding call. The male is the only large black bird with a bright-yellow head. He gives an impressive mating display, flying with his head drooped and feet and tail pointing down while steadily beating his wings. Young keep low and out of sight for up to three weeks before they start to fly. Migrates in large flocks of as many as 200 birds, often with Red-winged Blackbirds and Brown-headed Cowbirds. Flocks of mainly males return in first; females return later. Most colonies consist of 20–100 nests.

Killdeer
Charadrius vociferus

YEAR-ROUND

Size: 11" (28 cm)

Male: Upland shorebird with 2 black bands around the neck, like a necklace. Brown back and white belly. Bright reddish-orange rump, visible in flight.

Female: same as male

Juvenile: similar to adults, with a single neck band

Nest: ground; male scrapes; 2 broods per year

Eggs: 3–5; tan with brown markings

Incubation: 24–28 days; male and female incubate

Fledging: 25 days; male and female lead their young to food

Migration: non-migrator in Nevada; moves around to find food

Food: insects, worms, snails

Compare: The Spotted Sandpiper (p. 133) is found around water but lacks the 2 neck bands of the Killdeer.

Stan's Notes: Technically classified as a shorebird but lives in dry habitats instead of the shore. Often found in vacant fields, gravel pits, driveways, wetland edges, or along railroad tracks. The only shorebird that has two black neck bands. Known to fake a broken wing to draw intruders away from the nest; once the nest is safe, the parent will take flight. Nests are just a slight depression in a dry area and are often hard to see. Hatchlings look like miniature adults walking on stilts. Soon after hatching, the young follow their parents around and peck for insects. Gives a loud and distinctive "kill-deer" call. Migrates in small flocks.

red-shafted
male

red-shafted
female

yellow-shafted
male

yellow-shafted
female

Northern Flicker
Colaptes auratus

YEAR-ROUND

Size: 12" (30 cm)

Male: Brown and black with a red mustache and black necklace. Speckled chest. Gray head with a brown cap. Large white rump patch, seen only when flying.

Female: same as male but without a red mustache

Juvenile: same as adult of the same sex

Nest: cavity; female and male excavate; 1 brood per year

Eggs: 5–8; white without markings

Incubation: 11–14 days; female and male incubate

Fledging: 25–28 days; female and male feed the young

Migration: non-migrator in Nevada; moves around in winter

Food: insects (especially ants and beetles); comes to suet feeders

Compare: Female Williamson's Sapsucker (p. 51) has a finely barred back with a yellow belly and lacks Flicker's black spots on chest and belly.

Stan's Notes: This is the only woodpecker to regularly feed on the ground. Prefers ants and beetles and produces an antacid saliva that neutralizes the acidic defense of ants. Can be attracted to your yard with a nest box stuffed with sawdust. Yellow-shafted variety has golden-yellow wing linings and tails. Male yellow-shafteds have black mustaches; male red-shafteds have red mustaches. Hybrids between varieties occur in the Great Plains, where ranges overlap. Often reuses an old nest. Undulates deeply during flight, flashing yellow under its wings and tail and calling "wacka-wacka" loudly.

Mourning Dove
Zenaida macroura

YEAR-ROUND

Size: 12" (30 cm)

Male: Smooth and fawn-colored. Gray patch on the head. Iridescent pink and greenish blue on the neck. Black spot behind and below the eyes. Black spots on the wings and tail. Pointed, wedged tail; white edges seen in flight.

Female: similar to male, but lacks the pink-and-green iridescent neck feathers

Juvenile: spotted and streaked plumage

Nest: platform; female and male build; 2 broods per year

Eggs: 2; white without markings

Incubation: 13–14 days; male incubates during the day, female incubates at night

Fledging: 12–14 days; female and male feed the young

Migration: non-migrator to partial migrator; will move around to find food

Food: seeds; will visit seed and ground feeders

Compare: Eurasian Collared-Dove (p. 261) has a black collar on the nape of its neck. Rock Pigeon (p. 263) is larger and has a wide range of color combinations.

Stan's Notes: Name comes from its mournful cooing. A ground feeder, bobbing its head as it walks. One of the few birds to drink without lifting its head, like the Rock Pigeon. The parents feed the young (squab) a regurgitated liquid called crop-milk for their first few days of life. Platform nest is flimsy and often falls apart in storms. During takeoff and in flight, wind rushes through the bird's wing feathers, creating a characteristic whistling sound.

winter

breeding

Pied-billed Grebe
Podilymbus podiceps

YEAR-ROUND

Size: 12–14" (30–36 cm)

Male: Small and brown with a black chin and fluffy white patch beneath the tail. Black ring around a thick, chicken-like, ivory bill. Winter bill is brown and unmarked.

Female: same as male

Juvenile: paler than adults, with white spots and a gray chest, belly, and bill

Nest: floating platform; female and male build; 1–2 broods per year

Eggs: 5–7; bluish white without markings

Incubation: 22–24 days; female and male incubate

Fledging: 45–60 days; female and male feed the young

Migration: complete, to the Southwest, Mexico, Central America; non-migrator in most of Nevada

Food: crayfish, aquatic insects, fish

Compare: Look for a puffy white patch under the tail and thick, chicken-like bill to help identify.

Stan's Notes: A common resident water bird, often seen diving for food. When disturbed, it slowly sinks like a submarine, quickly compressing its feathers, forcing the air out. Was called Hell-diver due to the length of time it can stay submerged. Able to surface far from where it went under. Well suited to life on water, with short wings, lobed toes, and legs set close to the rear of its body. Swims easily but moves awkwardly on land. Very sensitive to pollution. Builds nest on a floating mat in water. "Grebe" may originate from the Breton word *krib*, meaning "crest," referring to the crested head plumes of many grebes, especially during breeding season.

male
p. 53

female

Bufflehead
Bucephala albeola

WINTER

Size: 13–15" (33–38 cm)

Female: Brownish-gray duck with a dark-brown head. White patch on cheek, just behind the eyes.

Male: striking black-and-white duck with a large bonnet-like white patch on the back of head; head shines greenish purple in sunlight

Juvenile: similar to female

Nest: cavity; female lines an old woodpecker cavity; 1 brood per year

Eggs: 8–10; ivory-to-olive without markings

Incubation: 29–31 days; female incubates

Fledging: 50–55 days; female leads the young to food

Migration: complete, to Nevada, Arizona, and New Mexico

Food: aquatic insects, crustaceans, mollusks

Compare: The female Common Goldeneye (p. 181) is very similar, but it is much larger and has a white collar. Look for the white cheek patch to help identify the female Bufflehead.

Stan's Notes: A small, common diving duck, almost always seen in small groups or with other duck species on rivers, ponds, and lakes. Nests in vacant woodpecker holes. When cavities in trees are scarce, known to use a burrow in an earthen bank or will use a nest box. Lines the cavity with fluffy down feathers. Unlike other ducks, the young stay in the nest for up to two days before they venture out with their mothers. The female is very territorial and remains with the same mate for many years.

breeding

winter
p. 267

displaying

Willet
Tringa semipalmata

Size: 14–16" (36–40 cm)

Male: Brown breeding plumage with a white belly. Brown bill and legs. Distinctive black-and-white wing lining pattern, seen in flight or during display.

Female: same as male

Juvenile: similar to breeding adult, more tan in color

Nest: ground; female and male build; 1 brood per year

Eggs: 3–5; olive-green with dark markings

Incubation: 24–28 days; male and female incubate

Fledging: 1–2 days; female and male feed young

Migration: complete, to parts of California, the coast of Mexico, and Central and South America

Food: insects, small fish, crabs, worms, clams

Compare: Larger than Spotted Sandpiper (p. 133). Killdeer (p. 149) has 2 black neck bands. Look for the long dark legs of the Willet.

Stan's Notes: It appears a rich, warm brown during the breeding season and rather plain gray during the winter, but it always has a striking black-and-white wing pattern when seen in flight. Uses its black-and-white wing patches to display to its mate. Named after the "pill-will-willet" call it gives during the breeding season. Gives a "kip-kip-kip" alarm call when it takes flight. It nests in far northeastern California, other western states, along the East Coast and in Canada.

female

male
p. 37

Great-tailed Grackle
Quiscalus mexicanus

YEAR-ROUND
SUMMER

Size: 15" (38 cm), female
18" (45 cm), male

Female: An overall brown bird with a gray-to-brown belly. Light-brown-to-white eyes, eyebrows, throat, and upper portion of chest.

Male: all-black bird with iridescent purple sheen on head and back, exceptionally long tail, bright-yellow eyes

Juvenile: similar to female

Nest: cup; female builds; 1–2 broods per year

Eggs: 3–5; greenish blue with brown markings

Incubation: 12–14 days; female incubates

Fledging: 21–23 days; female feeds young

Migration: partial migrator; moves around to find food; non-migrator in parts of Nevada

Food: insects, fruit, seeds; comes to seed feeders

Compare: Female Brewer's Blackbird (p. 139) is much smaller and has a darker-brown chest. Look for Great-tailed Grackle's distinct light-brown eyebrows.

Stan's Notes: This is our largest grackle. It was once considered a subspecies of the Boat-tailed Grackle, which occurs along the East Coast and Florida. A bird that prefers to nest near water in an open habitat. A colony nester. Males do not participate in nest building, incubation, or raising young. Males rarely fight; females squabble over nest sites and materials. Several females mate with one male. They are expanding northward, moving into northern states. Western populations tend to be larger than the eastern. Song varies from population to population.

soaring

Prairie Falcon

Falco mexicanus

YEAR-ROUND

Size: 15–16" (38–40 cm), male
16–18" (40–45 cm), female

Male: Thin body with a pale brown head, back, and tail. White breast and underwings, completely covered with small brown spots. Large squared head with a white area behind the eyes. Dark narrow mustache markings. Yellow base of bill, eye-rings, legs, and feet.

Female: similar to male, but noticeably larger

Juvenile: overall darker than adults, heavy vertical streaks on breast and belly

Nest: ground; both parents build; 1 brood per year

Eggs: 4–5; white with brown markings

Incubation: 29–31 days; male and female incubate

Fledging: 35–42 days; male and female feed young

Migration: partial to non-migrator; moves around in winter to find food

Food: birds, insects, small mammals, and reptiles

Compare: Peregrine Falcon (p. 273) is slightly larger, overall darker, with a black hood and wider mustache marks.

Stan's Notes: This is a falcon of open prairies, often wandering and showing up in unusual places during migration and winter. During courtship the male performs a strutting display for the female on the edge of the nest, along with spectacular aerial displays, all while calling to her. Perches on telephone poles, and cliffs, or hovers in search of prey. Jumps from a perch in a burst of rapid flight to overtake birds flying low to the ground. When soaring it will dive from high up, knocking small birds out of the sky to the ground in the same manner as the Peregrine Falcon.

163

winter male

male

female

Ruddy Duck

Oxyura jamaicensis

Size: 15" (38 cm)

Male: Compact reddish brown body. Black crown and nape. Large bright-white cheek patch. Distinctive light-blue bill. Long tail, often raised above water. Winter has a dull brown-to-gray body and dark bill.

Female: similar to winter male, lacks the large white cheek patch and blue bill

Juvenile: similar to female

Nest: ground; female builds; 1 brood per year

Eggs: 6–8; white without markings

Incubation: 23–26 days; female incubates

Fledging: 42–48 days; female and male feed young

Migration: partial to non-migrator; moves to find food

Food: aquatic insects and plants

Compare: Male Common Goldeneye (p. 59) has mostly white sides and a green head. Female Goldeneye (p. 181) has bright yellow eyes and a light gray body. Male Ring-necked Duck (p. 57) has gray sides and a white ring around the bill.

Stan's Notes: A diving duck with a unique appearance. Awkward on land. Often secretive, found on ponds and bays. Flushes quickly and stays away for a long time. Breeding male displays like a windup toy, ratcheting his head up and down, making muffled sounds and a staccato "pop." Male breeds with more than one female. Female lays some eggs in other duck nests. Male often seen with female and ducklings, but is not the father. Babies can dive soon after hatching. Has a blue bill, but is not the species that duck hunters call Blue Bill.

male

female

Green-winged Teal

Anas crecca

YEAR-ROUND
WINTER

Size: 14–15" (36–38 cm)

Male: Chestnut head with a dark-green patch out-lined with white from the eyes to the nape of neck. Gray body and butter-yellow tail. Green patch on the wings (speculum), seen in flight.

Female: light-brown duck with black spots and a green speculum, small bill

Juvenile: same as female

Nest: ground; female builds; 1 brood per year

Eggs: 8–10; cream-white without markings

Incubation: 21–23 days; female incubates

Fledging: 32–34 days; female teaches the young to feed

Migration: non-migrator to partial; many move around to find food

Food: aquatic plants and insects

Compare: Female Blue-winged Teal (p. 169) is similar in size, but it is slightly white at the base of its bill.

Stan's Notes: One of the smallest dabbling ducks. Tips forward in water to feed off the bottom of shallow ponds. This behavior makes it vulnerable to ingesting spent lead shot, which can cause death. It walks well on land and will also feed in flooded fields and woodlands. Known for its fast and agile flight. Groups wheel and spin through the air in tight formation. The green wing patches are most obvious during flight.

male

female

SUMMER

Blue-winged Teal
Spatula discors

Size: 15–16" (38–41 cm)

Male: Small, plain-looking brown duck with black speckles and a large, crescent-shaped white mark at the base of the bill. Gray head. Black tail with a small white patch. Blue wing patch (speculum), best seen in flight.

Female: duller than male, with only slight white at the base of the bill; lacks a crescent mark on the face and a white patch on the tail

Juvenile: same as female

Nest: ground; female builds; 1 brood per year

Eggs: 8–11; creamy white

Incubation: 23–27 days; female incubates

Fledging: 35–44 days; female feeds the young

Migration: complete, to New Mexico, Arizona, and Mexico,

Food: aquatic plants, seeds, aquatic insects

Compare: The female Mallard (p. 189) has an orange-and-black bill. Female Green-winged Teal (p. 167) is similar in size but lacks white at base of bill. Look for the white facial mark to identify the male Blue-winged.

Stan's Notes: An early migrator in Nevada. Most breeding birds here leave before other more northern ducks pass through in autumn. One of the smallest ducks in North America and one of the longest-distance migrating ducks, with widespread nesting as far north as Alaska. Constructs nest some distance from water. Female performs a distraction display to protect nest and young. Male leaves female near the end of incubation. Planting crops and cultivating to pond edges have caused a decline in population.

male

female

SUMMER

Cinnamon Teal
Spatula cyanoptera

Size: 16" (40 cm)

Male: Deep cinnamon head, neck, and belly. Light-brown back. Dark-gray bill. Deep-red eyes. Non-breeding male is overall brown with a red tinge.

Female: overall brown with a pale-brown head, long shovel-like bill, sky blue patch on wings

Juvenile: similar to female

Nest: ground; female builds; 1 brood per year

Eggs: 7–12; pinkish white without markings

Incubation: 21–25 days; female incubates

Fledging: 40–50 days; female teaches young to feed

Migration: complete migrator; to Arizona, Texas, and Mexico

Food: aquatic plants and insects, seeds

Compare: Male Teal shares the cinnamon sides of the larger male Northern Shoveler (p. 299), but lacks Shoveler's green head and very large spoon-shaped bill. Female Cinnamon Teal looks very similar to the smaller female Green-winged Teal (p. 167), which has a dark line through the eyes.

Stan's Notes: The male is one of the most stunningly beautiful ducks. When threatened, the female feigns a wing injury to lure the predator away from her young. Prefers to nest along alkaline marshes and shallow lakes, within 75 yards (68 m) of the water. Mallards and other ducks often lay eggs in teal nests, resulting in many nests with over 15 eggs.

male p. 55

female

Lesser Scaup

Aythya affinis

YEAR-ROUND
MIGRATION
WINTER

Size: 16–17" (40–43 cm)

Female: Overall brown duck with a dull-white patch at the base of a light-gray bill. Yellow eyes.

Male: white and gray; the chest and head appear nearly black, but the head looks purple with green highlights in direct sun; yellow eyes

Juvenile: same as female

Nest: ground; female builds; 1 brood per year

Eggs: 8–14; olive-buff without markings

Incubation: 22–28 days; female incubates

Fledging: 45–50 days; female teaches young to feed

Migration: complete, to California, Arizona, New Mexico, Texas, and Mexico

Food: aquatic plants and insects

Compare: Female Ring-necked Duck (p. 177) is a similar size but has a white ring around the bill. Male Blue-winged Teal (p. 169) is slightly smaller and has a crescent-shaped white mark at base of bill.

Stan's Notes: A common diving duck. Often seen in large flocks on lakes, ponds and sewage lagoons. Submerges itself completely to feed on the bottom of lakes (unlike dabbling ducks, which only tip forward to reach the bottom). Note the bold white stripe under the wings when in flight. The male leaves the female when she starts incubating eggs. The quantity of eggs (clutch size) increases with the female's age. This species has an interesting babysitting arrangement in which groups of young (crèches) are tended by one to three adult females.

Barn Owl
Tyto alba

YEAR-ROUND

Size: 16–19" (40–48 cm); up to 4' wingspan

Male: "Non-eared" owl with a rusty-brown back of head, back, wings, and tail. Heart-shaped white face, outlined in darker rusty brown. White chest and belly. Dark eyes. Long gray legs. Gray feet. Yellow bill.

Female: similar to male, often with a rusty wash over the chest and belly

Juvenile: light gray to white; fuzzy-looking overall

Nest: cavity, occasionally on a cliff; female builds; 1–2 broods per year

Eggs: 3–7; white without markings

Incubation: 30–34 days; female incubates

Fledging: 52–56 days; male and female feed the young

Migration: non-migrator

Food: small mammals, birds, snakes

Compare: Burrowing Owl (p. 143) is smaller and lacks the heart-shaped face of the Barn Owl. The Western Screech-Owl (p. 247) is smaller, has ear tufts, and lacks the white face of the Barn Owl.

Stan's Notes: This owl is well known for nesting in old barns (hence the common name) but will also nest in any dark cavity, on cliffs, or in trees. The male feeds the female during incubation. Clutch size depends on availability of prey: the more prey, the larger the clutch. Young hatch one per day (asynchronously) over two weeks, creating a range of ages in the nest. Will sway back and forth with lowered head when confronted.

male p. 57

female

Ring-necked Duck

Aythya collaris

Size: 16–19" (41–48 cm)

Female: Brown with a darker brown back and crown and lighter-brown sides. Gray face. White eye-ring with a white line behind the eye. White ring around the bill. Peaked head.

Male: black head, chest, and back; gray-to-white sides; blue bill with a bold white ring and a thinner ring at the base; peaked head

Juvenile: similar to female

Nest: ground; female builds; 1 brood per year

Eggs: 8–10; olive to brown without markings

Incubation: 26–27 days; female incubates

Fledging: 49–56 days; female teaches the young to feed

Migration: complete, to Nevada and southwestern states; non-migrator in parts of the state

Food: aquatic plants and insects

Compare: Look for the white ring around the bill to help identify the female Ring-necked Duck.

Stan's Notes: Often seen in larger freshwater lakes, usually in small flocks or just pairs. A diving duck, watch for it to dive underwater to forage for food. Springs up off the water to take flight. Has a distinctive tall, peaked head with a sloped forehead. Flattens its crown when diving. Male gives a quick series of grating barks and grunts. Female gives high-pitched peeps. Named "Ring-necked" for its cinnamon collar, which is nearly impossible to see in the field. Also called Ring-billed Duck due to the white ring on its bill.

male

female

American Wigeon
Mareca americana

YEAR-ROUND
MIGRATION
WINTER

Size: 18–20" (48 cm)

Male: Brown duck with a rounded head and obvious white cap. Deep-green patch starting behind the eyes and streaking down the neck. Long pointed tail. Short, black-tipped grayish bill. White belly and wing linings, seen in flight. Non-breeding lacks white cap and green patch.

Female: light brown with a pale-gray head, a short black-tipped grayish bill, green wing patch (speculum), and dark eye spot; white belly and wing linings, seen in flight

Juvenile: similar to female

Nest: ground; female builds; 1 brood per year

Eggs: 7–12; white without markings

Incubation: 23–25 days; female incubates

Fledging: 37–48 days; female teaches the young to feed

Migration: complete, to Arizona, New Mexico, Texas, and Mexico; non-migrator in parts of Nevada

Food: aquatic plants, seeds

Compare: Male American Wigeon is easily identified by the white cap and black-tipped grayish bill. Look for the black-tipped grayish bill and green wing patch to help identify the female American Wigeon.

Stan's Notes: Often in small flocks or with other ducks. Prefers shallow lakes. Male stays with the female only during the first week of incubation. Female raises the young. If threatened, female feigns injury while the young run and hide. Conceals nest in tall vegetation within 50–250 yards (46–229 m) of water.

male
p. 59

female

Common Goldeneye

Bucephala clangula

WINTER

Size: 18–20" (45–51 cm)

Female: Brown and gray duck with a large dark-brown head and gray body. White collar. Bright-golden eyes. Yellow-tipped dark bill.

Male: mostly white with a black back, a puffy green head, a large white spot on the face, bright-golden eyes, and a dark bill

Juvenile: same as female but with a dark bill

Nest: cavity; female lines an old woodpecker cavity; 1 brood per year

Eggs: 8–10; bluish to olive green without markings

Incubation: 28–32 days; female incubates

Fledging: 56–59 days; female leads the young to food

Migration: complete, to Nevada, other southwestern states, and Mexico

Food: aquatic plants, insects, fish, mollusks

Compare: Similar size as female Redhead (p. 183), which is uniformly light brown, lacking the gray body of female Goldeneye. Look for the dark-brown head, white collar, and golden-yellow eyes to help identify the female Common Goldeneye.

Stan's Notes: Known for the loud whistling sound produced by its wings during flight. During late winter and early spring, the male performs elaborate mating displays that include throwing his head back and calling a raspy note. Female will lay some of her eggs in other goldeneye nests or in the nests of other species (egg dumping), causing some mothers to incubate as many as 30 eggs in a brood. Named for its bright-golden eyes. Winters in Nevada where it finds open water.

male p. 313

female

Redhead
Aythya americana

SUMMER
WINTER

Size: 19" (48 cm)

Female: Soft-brown, plain-looking duck with gray-to-white wing linings. Rounded top of head. Two-toned bill, gray with a black tip.

Male: rich-red head and neck with a black chest and tail, gray sides, smoky-gray wings and back, tricolored bill with a light-blue base, white ring, and black tip

Juvenile: similar to female

Nest: cup; female builds; 1 brood per year

Eggs: 9–14; pale white without markings

Incubation: 24–28 days; female incubates

Fledging: 56–73 days; female shows young what to eat

Migration: complete migrator, to southwestern state, Mexico, and Central America

Food: seeds, aquatic plants, insects

Compare: Female Northern Shoveler (p. 187) is similar, but it is lighter brown and has an exceptionally large, shovel-shaped bill.

Stan's Notes: A duck of permanent large bodies of water. Forages along the shoreline, feeding on seeds, aquatic plants, and insects. Usually builds nest directly on the water's surface, using large mats of vegetation. Female lays up to 75 percent of its eggs in the nests of other Redheads and several other duck species. Nests primarily in the Prairie Pothole region of the northern Great Plains. Overall populations seem to be increasing at about 2–3 percent each year.

male
p. 277

female

Gadwall

Mareca strepera

YEAR-ROUND
SUMMER
WINTER

Size: 19" (48 cm)

Female: Mottled brown with a pronounced color change from dark-brown body to light-brown neck and head. Bright-white wing linings, seen in flight. Small white wing patch, seen when swimming. Gray bill with orange sides.

Male: plump gray duck with a brown head and distinctive black rump, white belly, bright-white wing linings, small white wing patch, chestnut-tinged wings, gray bill

Juvenile: similar to female

Nest: ground; female lines the nest with fine grass and down feathers plucked from her chest; 1 brood per year

Eggs: 8–11; white without markings

Incubation: 24–27 days; female incubates

Fledging: 48–56 days; young feed themselves

Migration: complete, to southwestern states, Mexico; a few remain in winter in Nevada

Food: aquatic insects and plants

Compare: Female Mallard (p. 189) is similar but has a blue-and-white wing mark. Look for Gadwall's white wing patch and gray bill with orange sides.

Stan's Notes: A duck of shallow marshes. Consumes mostly plant material, dunking its head in water to feed rather than tipping forward, like other dabbling ducks. Walks well on land; feeds in fields and woodlands. Nests within 300 feet (90 m) of water. Often in pairs with other duck species. Establishes pair bond during winter.

185

male p. 299

female

Northern Shoveler
Spatula clypeata

YEAR-ROUND
SUMMER
WINTER

Size: 19–21" (48–53 cm)

Female: A medium-sized brown duck speckled with black. Green patch on the wings (speculum). An extraordinarily large, spoon-shaped bill.

Male: iridescent green head, rusty sides, white chest, and a large spoon-shaped bill

Juvenile: same as female

Nest: ground; female builds; 1 brood per year

Eggs: 9–12; olive without markings

Incubation: 22–25 days; female incubates

Fledging: 30–60 days; female leads the young to food

Migration: complete, to Arizona, New Mexico, Mexico, and Central America; non-migrator in parts of Nevada

Food: aquatic insects, plants

Compare: Female Mallard (p. 189) is similar but lacks the Shoveler's large bill. Female Redhead (p. 183) is overall lighter brown and has a dark gray bill with a black tip. Look for Shoveler's large spoon-shaped bill to help identify.

Stan's Notes: One of several species of shovelers. Called "Shoveler" due to the peculiar, shovel-like shape of its bill. Given the common name "Northern" because it is the only species of these ducks in North America. Seen in shallow wetlands, ponds and small lakes in flocks of 5–10 birds. Flocks fly in tight formation. Swims low in water, pointing its large bill toward the water as if it's too heavy to lift. Usually swims in tight circles while feeding. Feeds mainly by filtering tiny aquatic insects and plants from the surface of the water with its bill.

male
p. 297

female

Mallard
Anas platyrhynchos

YEAR-ROUND

Size: 19–21" (48–53 cm)

Female: Brown duck with a blue-and-white wing mark (speculum). Orange-and-black bill.

Male: large green head, white necklace, rust-brown or chestnut chest, combination of gray-and-white sides, yellow bill, orange legs and feet

Juvenile: same as female but with a yellow bill

Nest: ground; female builds; 1 brood per year

Eggs: 7–10; greenish to whitish, unmarked

Incubation: 26–30 days; female incubates

Fledging: 42–52 days; female leads the young to food

Migration: non-migrator to partial migrator in Nevada

Food: seeds, plants, aquatic insects; will come to ground feeders offering corn

Compare: Female Gadwall (p. 185) has a gray bill with orange sides. Female Northern Pintail (p. 191) is similar to female Mallard, but it has a gray bill. Female Northern Shoveler (p. 187) has a spoon-shaped bill.

Stan's Notes: A familiar dabbling duck of lakes and ponds. Also found in rivers, streams and some backyards. Tips forward to feed on vegetation on the bottom of shallow water. The name "Mallard" comes from the Latin word *masculus,* meaning "male," referring to the male's habit of taking no part in raising the young. Female and male have white underwings and white tails, but only the male has black central tail feathers that curl upward. The female gives a classic quack. Returns to its birthplace each year.

male

female

Northern Pintail

Anas acuta

Size: 20" (52 cm), female
25" (63 cm), male

Male: A slender, elegant duck with a brown head, white neck, and gray body. Gray bill. Extremely long and narrow black tail. Non-breeding has a pale-brown head that lacks the clear demarcation between the brown head and white neck. Lacks long tail feathers.

Female: mottled brown body with a paler head and neck, long tail, gray bill

Juvenile: similar to female

Nest: ground; female builds; 1 brood per year

Eggs: 6–9; olive-green without markings

Incubation: 22–25 days; female incubates

Fledging: 36–50 days; female teaches young to feed

Migration: non-migrator to partial, to southwestern states and Mexico; non-migrator in parts of Nevada

Food: aquatic plants and insects, seeds

Compare: The male Northern Pintail has a distinctive brown head and white neck and unique long tail feathers. Female Mallard (p. 189) is similar to female Pintail, but Mallard has an orange bill with black spots.

Stan's Notes: A common dabbling duck of marshes in the winter. About 90 percent of its diet is aquatic plants, except when females feed heavily on aquatic insects prior to nesting, presumably to gain extra nutrients for egg production. Male holds tail upright from the water's surface. No other North American duck has such a long tail.

male
p. 275

female

soaring

Northern Harrier
Circus hudsonius

YEAR-ROUND
WINTER

Size: 18–22" (45–56 cm); up to 4' wingspan

Female: Slender, low-flying hawk with a dark-brown back and brown streaking on the chest and belly. Large white rump patch. Thin black tail bands and black wing tips. Yellow eyes.

Male: silver-gray with a large white rump patch and white belly, black wing tips, yellow eyes, faint thin bands across the tail

Juvenile: similar to female, with an orange breast

Nest: ground; female and male construct; 1 brood per year

Eggs: 4–8; bluish white without markings

Incubation: 31–32 days; female incubates

Fledging: 30–35 days; male and female feed the young

Migration: partial migrator, to southwestern states, Mexico, and Central America; non-migrator in much of Nevada

Food: mice, snakes, insects, small birds

Compare: Slimmer than the Red-tailed Hawk (p. 199). Look for the characteristic low gliding and the black tail bands to identify the female Harrier.

Stan's Notes: One of the easiest of hawks to identify. Glides just above the ground, following the contours of the land while searching for prey. Holds its wings just above horizontal, tilting back and forth in the wind, similar to the Turkey Vulture. Formerly called Marsh Hawk due to its habit of hunting over marshes. Feeds and nests on the ground. Will also preen and rest on the ground. Unlike other hawks, mainly uses its hearing to find prey, followed by its sight. At any age, it has a distinctive owl-like face disk.

juvenile

adult soaring

juvenile soaring

light morph

juvenile

adult soaring

juvenile soaring

dark morph

Rough-legged Hawk

Buteo lagopus

Size: 18–23" (56 cm); up to 4½' wingspan

Male: A hawk of several plumages. All plumages have a long tail with a dark band or bands. Distinctive dark wrists and belly. Relatively long wings, small bill and feet. Light morph has nearly pure white undersides of wings and base of tail. Dark morph is nearly all brown with light-gray trailing edge of wings.

Female: same as male, only larger

Juvenile: similar to adults

Nest: platform, on edge of cliff; female and male build; 1 brood per year

Eggs: 2–6; white with brown markings

Incubation: 28–31 days; female and male incubate

Fledging: 39–43 days; female and male feed young

Migration: complete, to Nevada

Food: small mammals, snakes, large insects

Compare: Red-tailed Hawk (p. 199) has a belly band and lacks dark "wrist" marks. Smaller than Swainson's Hawk (p. 197) which has dark trailing edges on the wings.

Stan's Notes: Two color morphs, light and dark, light being more common. A common winter resident and migrant in Nevada. Map reflects the combined range. More numerous in some years than others. It has much smaller and weaker feet than the other birds of prey, which means it must hunt smaller prey. Hunts from the air, usually hovering before diving for small rodents such as mice and voles.

soaring light morph

intermediate morph

light morph

dark morph

soaring dark morph

Swainson's Hawk
Buteo swainsoni

Size: 19–22" (48–56 cm); up to 4¾' wingspan

Male: Highly variable plumage with three easily distinguishable color morphs. Light morph is brown and has a white belly, warm rusty chest, and white face. Intermediate has a dark chest, rusty belly, and white at the base of bill. Dark morph is nearly all dark brown with a rusty color low on the belly.

Female: same as male

Juvenile: similar to adult

Nest: platform; female and male construct; 1 brood per year

Eggs: 2–4; bluish or white with some brown marks

Incubation: 28–35 days; female incubates

Fledging: 42–44 days; female and male feed young

Migration: complete, to Central and South America

Food: small mammals, insects, snakes, birds

Compare: Slimmer than Red-tailed Hawk (p. 199), which has a white chest and brown belly band. Ferruginous Hawk (p. 201) has a light trailing edge of wings.

Stan's Notes: A slender open country hawk that hunts mammals, insects, snakes and birds when soaring (kiting) or perching. Often flies with slightly upturned wings in a teetering, vulture-like flight. The light morph is the most common, but the intermediate and dark are also common. Even minor nest disturbance can cause nest failure. Often gathers in large flocks to migrate.

soaring

juvenile
soaring

juvenile

Red-tailed Hawk
Buteo jamaicensis

YEAR-ROUND

Size: 19–23" (48–63 cm); up to 4½' wingspan

Male: Variety of colorations, from chocolate brown to nearly all white. Often brown with a white breast and brown belly band. Rust-red tail. Underside of wing is white with a small dark patch on the leading edge near the shoulder.

Female: same as male but slightly larger

Juvenile: similar to adults, with a speckled breast and light eyes; lacks a red tail

Nest: platform; male and female build; 1 brood per year

Eggs: 2–3; white without markings or sometimes marked with brown

Incubation: 30–35 days; female and male incubate

Fledging: 45–46 days; male and female feed the young

Migration: non-migrator to partial migrator; moves around to find food

Food: small and medium-sized mammals, large birds, snakes, insects, bats, carrion

Compare: Swainson's Hawk (p. 197) is slimmer with longer, more pointed wings.

Stan's Notes: Common in open country and cities in Nevada. Seen perching on fences, freeway lampposts, and trees. Look for it circling above open fields and roadsides, searching for prey. Gives a high-pitched scream that trails off. Often builds a large stick nest in large trees along roads. Lines nest with finer material, like evergreen needles. Returns to the same nest site each year. The red tail develops in the second year and is best seen from above.

soaring

soaring
juvenile

juvenile

Ferruginous Hawk
Buteo regalis

YEAR-ROUND
SUMMER
MIGRATION
WINTER

Size: 22–26" (56–66 cm); up to 4' wingspan

Male: Pale brown head, gray cheeks, reddish back and white chin, chest, and belly. Rust flanks extend down feathered legs. Bright white undersides of wings, light rust wing linings. Tail white below, rust-tinged on top. Large, strong yellow feet. Red eyes. Dark eye line.

Female: same as male, but noticeably larger

Juvenile: brown head, nape, back, and wings with a white chin, chest, and belly

Nest: massive platform, low in a tree, sometimes on the ground; female and male construct; 1 brood per year

Eggs: 2–4; bluish or white, can have brown marks

Incubation: 28–33 days; female and male incubate

Fledging: 44–48 days; female and male feed young

Migration: complete, to southwestern states, Mexico; non-migrator in a small portion of Nevada

Food: larger mammals, snakes, insects, birds

Compare: Swainson's Hawk (p. 197) is smaller and has a dark trailing edge of wings. Red-tailed Hawk (p. 199) has a brown belly band and lacks rusty flanks and legs.

Stan's Notes: The largest hawk species. Found in western prairies. Common name means "iron-like," referring to the rusty color. Male and female perform aerial courtships, soaring with wings held above their backs, male diving at female, grabbing each other with large, powerful feet. Often hunts larger mammals such as jackrabbits. Often stands on the ground.

Great Horned Owl
Bubo virginianus

YEAR-ROUND

Size:	21–25" (53–64 cm); up to 4' wingspan
Male:	Robust brown "horned" owl. Bright-yellow eyes and a V-shaped white throat resembling a necklace. Horizontal barring on the chest.
Female:	same as male but slightly larger
Juvenile:	similar to adults but lacks ear tufts
Nest:	no nest; takes over the nest of a crow, hawk, or Great Blue Heron or uses a partial cavity, stump or broken tree; 1 brood per year
Eggs:	2–3; white without markings
Incubation:	26–30 days; female incubates
Fledging:	30–35 days; male and female feed the young
Migration:	non-migrator
Food:	mammals, birds (ducks), snakes, insects
Compare:	Burrowing Owl (p. 143) is much smaller and has long legs. Look for bright-yellow eyes and feather "horns" on the head to help identify the Great Horned Owl.

Stan's Notes: The largest owl in the state. One of the earliest nesting birds in Nevada, laying eggs in January and February. Able to hunt in complete darkness due to its excellent hearing. The "horns," or "ears," are tufts of feathers and have nothing to do with hearing. Cannot turn its head all the way around. Wing feathers are ragged on the ends, resulting in silent flight. Eyelids close from the top down, like humans. Fearless, it is one of the few animals that will kill skunks and porcupines. Given that, it is also called the Flying Tiger. Call sounds like "hoo-hoo-hoo-hoooo."

displaying

Greater Roadrunner
Geococcyx californianus

YEAR-ROUND

Size: 23" (58 cm)

Male: Overall brown with white streaking. Long, pointed brown bill. Extremely long tail. Blue patch just behind eyes. Short round wings are darker brown than body. Long gray legs with large feet. Has a conspicuous crest that can be raised and lowered.

Female: same as male

Juvenile: similar to adult

Nest: platform, low in a tree, shrub or cactus; the female and male build; 1–2 broods per year

Eggs: 4–6; white without markings

Incubation: 18–20 days; male and female incubate

Fledging: 16–18 days; male and female feed young

Migration: non-migrator

Food: insects, reptiles, small mammals and birds

Compare: This uniquely shaped ground dweller has an extremely long tail, a prominent crest, and is hard to confuse with other birds.

Stan's Notes: Ground dweller with a very long tail and prominent crest when raised. Cuckoo family member known to run quickly across the ground to catch prey. A formidable predator, able to run up to 15 miles (24 km) per hour. Flies short distances, usually in a low glide after a running takeoff. Raises its tail high, lowers it slowly. A slow, descending, low-pitched "coo-coo-coo-coo." Male does most incubating and feeding of young. Performs a distraction display to protect the nest. Young can catch prey four weeks after leaving the nest.

winter

breeding

in flight

White-faced Ibis
Plegadis chihi

Size: 23" (58 cm); up to 3' wingspan

Male: Appears brown with rusty-red (chestnut) on upper body. Glossy brown with green sheen on lower body. Long, down-curved gray bill. White border on a light red face. Orange-red legs and feet. Deep red eyes. Winter has a gray mask and less chestnut.

Female: same as male

Juvenile: similar to winter adult

Nest: platform, on ground, low in shrub or small tree; female and male build; 1 brood a year

Eggs: 2–4; blue or green

Incubation: 21–23 days; female and male incubate

Fledging: 30–35 days; female and male feed young

Migration: complete, to California and Mexico

Food: insects, crayfish, frogs, small fish, shellfish

Compare: American Avocet (p. 61) is mostly black and white with an upturned bill.

Stan's Notes: Of the three ibis species in the US, this is the only one regularly seen in Nevada. Usually found in marshes and estuaries. When near and in good light, appears glossy red with green, blue and purple highlights. Uses its long bill to find and eat aquatic insects and fish. Large groups fly in a straight line. Rapid, shallow wing beat, then a short glide. Nests close to the water in large colonies with egrets and herons. Builds a loose nest of thin twigs, leaves and roots, lined with green leaves. Male spends more time feeding young than the female. Common name comes from the white outline on face.

American Bittern
Botaurus lentiginosus

SUMMER
MIGRATION
WINTER

Size: 28" (71 cm)

Male: Overall brown with thick rusty striping on neck, chest, and belly. White chin. A unique shape with an extremely long neck, round compact body, and short tail. Green legs and feet. Long, pointed yellow bill. Golden eyes.

Female: same as male

Juvenile: similar to adult

Nest: ground; female builds; 1 brood per year

Eggs: 4–5; light brown without markings

Incubation: 28–29 days; female incubates

Fledging: 7–14 days; female feeds young

Migration: complete migrator in Nevada, to Arizona, New Mexico, and Mexico

Food: small fish, aquatic insects, amphibians

Compare: The Black-crowned Night-Heron (p. 65) is gray and white with a black cap and dark bill. Great Blue Heron (p. 281) is much larger and has grayish-blue plumage.

Stan's Notes: Very secretive bird that seems to be on the decline. Hunts by walking extremely slowly, looking for prey along edges of ponds, streams, and wetlands. Strikes an erect posture and points its large yellow bill straight up into the air to disguise itself. Carries this camouflage one step further, swaying back and forth in wind to match surrounding cattails and other aquatic vegetation (reeds). Strikes quickly at prey with its sharp bill. Usually solitary, roosting in trees at any hour. The male's loud booming call sounds like a slow water pump, hence its other common name, Slough-pumper.

Ring-necked Pheasant
Phasianus colchicus

YEAR-ROUND

Size: 30–36" (76–91 cm), male, including tail
21–25" (53–64 cm), female, including tail

Male: Golden-brown body with a long tail. White ring around the neck. Head is purple, green, blue, and red.

Female: smaller and less flamboyant than the male, with brown plumage and a long tail

Juvenile: similar to female, with a shorter tail

Nest: ground; female builds; 1 brood per year

Eggs: 8–10; olive-brown without markings

Incubation: 23–25 days; female incubates

Fledging: 11–12 days; female leads the young to food

Migration: non-migrator; moves around to find food

Food: insects, seeds, fruit; visits ground feeders

Compare: Larger than California Quail (p. 255) and Gambel's Quail (p. 257). Neither have the long narrow tail of the pheasant. Male Ring-necked is brightly colored.

Stan's Notes: Originally introduced to North America from China in the late 1800s. Common now throughout the US. Like many other game birds, its numbers vary greatly, making it common in some years, scarce in others. Seeks shelter during harsh winter weather. To attract females, the male gives a cackling call and then rapidly flutters his wings. Takes off in an explosive flight with fast wingbeats followed by gliding low to the ground. The name "Ring-necked" refers to the white ring around the male's neck. "Pheasant" comes from the Greek word *phaisianos*, which means "bird of the River Phasis" (known today as the Rioni River).

soaring

juvenile

juvenile

YEAR-ROUND

Golden Eagle
Aquila chrysaetos

Size: 30–40" (76–102 cm); up to 7¼' wingspan

Male: Uniform dark brown with a golden-yellow head and nape of neck. Yellow around base of bill. Yellow feet.

Female: same as male

Juvenile: similar to adult, with white "wrist" patches and a white base of tail

Nest: platform, on a cliff; female and male build; 1 brood per year

Eggs: 1–2; white with brown markings

Incubation: 43–45 days; female and male incubate

Fledging: 63–75 days; female and male feed young

Migration: non-migrator in Nevada, moves around to find food

Food: mammals, birds, reptiles, insects

Compare: The Bald Eagle (p. 69) adult is similar, but it has a white head and white tail. Bald Eagle juvenile is often confused with the Golden Eagle juvenile; both are large dark birds with white markings.

Stan's Notes: A large, powerful raptor that has no trouble taking larger prey such as jackrabbits. Hunts by perching or soaring and watching for movement. Inhabits mountainous terrain, requiring large territories to provide a large supply of food. Long-term pair bond, renewing its bond late in winter with spectacular high-flying courtship displays. Usually nests on cliff faces; rarely nests in trees. Uses a well-established nest that's been used for generations. Will add items to the nest such as antlers, bones, and barbed wire.

displaying male

non-displaying

female

Wild Turkey
Meleagris gallopavo

Size: 36–48" (91–122 cm)

Male: Large brown-and-bronze bird with a naked blue-and-red head. Long, straight, black beard in the center of the chest. Tail spreads open like a fan. Spurs on legs.

Female: thinner and less striking than the male; often lacks a breast beard

Juvenile: same as adult of the same sex

Nest: ground; female builds; 1 brood per year

Eggs: 10–12; buff-white with dull-brown markings

Incubation: 27–28 days; female incubates

Fledging: 6–10 days; female leads the young to food

Migration: non-migrator; moves around to find food

Food: insects, seeds, fruit

Compare: This bird is quite distinctive and unlikely to be confused with others.

Stan's Notes: The largest game bird in the state, and the species from which the domestic turkey was bred. A strong flier that can approach 60 miles (97 km) per hour. Can fly straight up, then away. Eyesight is three times better than ours. Hearing is also excellent; can hear competing males up to a mile away. Male has a "harem" of up to 20 females. Female scrapes out a shallow depression for nesting and pads it with soft leaves. Males are known as toms, females are hens, and young are poults. Roosts in trees at night.

Ruby-crowned Kinglet
Regulus calendula

YEAR-ROUND
SUMMER
WINTER

Size: 4" (10 cm)

Male: Small, teardrop-shaped green-to-gray bird. Two white wing bars and a white eye-ring. Hidden ruby crown.

Female: same as male, but lacks a ruby crown

Juvenile: same as female

Nest: pendulous; female builds; 1 brood per year

Eggs: 4–5; white with brown markings

Incubation: 11–12 days; female incubates

Fledging: 11–12 days; female and male feed the young

Migration: non-migrator to partial

Food: insects, berries

Compare: The female American Goldfinch (p. 325) shares the drab olive plumage and unmarked chest, but it is larger. Look for the white eye-ring to identify the Ruby-crowned Kinglet.

Stan's Notes: This is one of the smaller birds in the state. Look for it flitting around thick shrubs low to the ground. It takes a quick eye to see the ruby crown, which the male flashes when he is excited. The female weaves an unusually intricate nest and fastens colorful lichens and mosses to the exterior with spiderwebs. Often builds the nest high in a mature tree, where it hangs from a branch that has overlapping leaves. Sings a distinctive song that starts out soft and ends loud and on a higher note. "Kinglet" originates from the word *king*, referring to the male's red crown, and the diminutive suffix *let*, meaning "small."

male

female

YEAR-ROUND
WINTER

Golden-crowned Kinglet
Regulus satrapa

Size: 4" (10 cm)

Male: Tiny, plump green-to-gray bird. Distinctive yellow-and-orange patch with a black border on the crown (top inset). White eyebrow mark. 2 white wing bars.

Female: same as male, but has a yellow crown with a black border, lacks any orange (bottom inset)

Juvenile: same as adults, but lacks gold on crown

Nest: pendulous; female builds; 1–2 broods per year

Eggs: 5–9; white or creamy with brown markings

Incubation: 14–15 days; female incubates

Fledging: 14–19 days; female and male feed the young

Migration: non-migrator to partial, moves around to find food in winter

Food: insects, fruit, tree sap

Compare: Similar to the Ruby-crowned Kinglet (p. 217), but the Golden-crowned has an obvious crown. Female American Goldfinch (p. 325) is larger and has an all-black forehead.

Stan's Notes: Often seen in flocks with chickadees, nuthatches, woodpeckers, and Ruby-crowned Kinglets. Flicks its wings when moving around. Constructs an unusual hanging nest, often with moss, lichens and spiderwebs, and lines it with bark and feathers. Can have so many eggs in its small nest that eggs are in two layers. Drinks tree sap and feeds by gleaning insects from trees. Can be very tame and approachable but constantly on the move.

male

female

Red-breasted Nuthatch
Sitta canadensis

YEAR-ROUND WINTER

Size: 4½" (11 cm)

Male: Gray-backed bird with an obvious black eye line and black cap. Rust-red breast and belly.

Female: duller than male and has a gray cap and pale undersides

Juvenile: same as female

Nest: cavity; male and female excavate a cavity or move into a vacant hole; 1 brood per year

Eggs: 5–6; white with red-brown markings

Incubation: 11–12 days; female incubates

Fledging: 14–20 days; female and male feed the young

Migration: non-migrator to irruptive; moves around the state in search of food

Food: insects, insect eggs, seeds; comes to seed and suet feeders

Compare: White-breasted Nuthatch (p. 233) is larger, and does not have the rust-red breast and black eye line of Red-breasted Nuthatch.

Stan's Notes: The nuthatch climbs down trunks of trees headfirst, searching for insects. Like a chickadee, it grabs a seed from a feeder and flies off to crack it open. It wedges the seed into a crevice and pounds it open with several sharp blows. The name "Nuthatch" comes from the Middle English moniker *nuthak*, referring to the habit of hacking seeds open. Look for it in mature conifers, where it extracts seeds from pine cones. Excavates a cavity or takes an old woodpecker hole or a natural cavity and builds a nest within. Gives a series of nasal "yank-yank-yank" calls.

Bushtit
Psaltriparus minimus

Size: 4½" (11 cm)

Male: Overall dull gray bird with a relatively long tail. Black eyes and legs. Tiny black bill.

Female: same as male, but has pale yellow eyes

Juvenile: similar to adults, with dark brown eyes

Nest: pendulous; female and male construct; 1–2 broods per year

Eggs: 5–7; white without markings

Incubation: 10–12 days; female and male incubate

Fledging: 14–15 days; female and male feed young

Migration: non-migrator

Food: insects, seeds, fruit; comes to seed feeders

Compare: Smaller than Black-capped and Mountain Chickadees (pp. 227 and 229) and lacks the black caps and white on the face of the Chickadees.

Stan's Notes: A lively bird, often seen in extended family flocks of up to 20 individuals in open woods and low woodlands. Often seen with other species of birds such as kinglets, wrens, and chickadees. Easily picked out by its small size, long tail and the extremely short bill. Groups will roost together, huddling tightly to keep warm and save energy. Eyes are pale yellow in adult females, dark brown in juveniles, and black in adult males.

male

juvenile

female

YEAR-ROUND

Verdin
Auriparus flaviceps

Size: 4½" (11 cm)

Male: Light gray to silvery overall. Lemon-yellow head. Rusty-red shoulder patch, frequently hidden. Short, pointed dark bill. Dark mark between bill and eyes. Dark legs and feet.

Female: duller than male

Juvenile: overall gray, lacks the yellow head, dark bill, and rusty-red shoulder patch

Nest: covered cup; male builds; 1–2 broods a year

Eggs: 4–5; bluish green with brown markings

Incubation: 8–10 days; female incubates

Fledging: 19–21 days; female and male feed young

Migration: non-migrator

Food: seeds, insects, fruit, nectar; comes to nectar feeders and orange halves

Compare: Mountain Chickadee (p. 229) has an obvious black cap, chin, and eye line.

Stan's Notes: A very friendly bird that can be a regular visitor to nectar feeders and orange halves. Often hides its rusty-red shoulder marks, confusing the novice bird watcher. Most easily identified as a tiny gray bird with a yellow head. Male builds several ball-shaped, conspicuous nests of thorny twigs, interweaves them with leaves and grass, and lines them with feathers and plant down. Male shows the nest possibilities to female and she selects one. After fledging, young return to nest at night, unlike most small birds, which leave and don't return for shelter. Often uses nest for several seasons.

YEAR-ROUND

Black-capped Chickadee
Poecile atricapillus

Size: 5" (13 cm)

Male: Familiar gray bird with a black cap and throat patch. Tan sides and belly. White chest. Small white wing marks.

Female: same as male

Juvenile: same as adult

Nest: cavity; female and male excavate or use a nest box; 1 brood per year

Eggs: 5–7; white with fine brown markings

Incubation: 11–13 days; female incubates

Fledging: 14–18 days; female and male feed the young

Migration: non-migrator

Food: insects, seeds, fruit; comes to seed and suet feeders

Compare: The Mountain Chickadee (p. 229) has white eyebrows. Larger than the Bushtit (p. 223), which lacks the Black-capped's black cap and white on face.

Stan's Notes: A perky backyard bird that can be attracted with a nest box or bird feeder. Usually the first to find a new seed or suet feeder. Can be easily tamed and hand-fed. Much of the diet comes from bird feeders, so it can be a common urban bird. Needs to feed every day in winter, and forages to find food even during the worst winter storms. Typically seen with nuthatches, woodpeckers, and other birds. Builds nest mostly with green moss and lines it with fur. Named "Chickadee" for its familiar "chika-dee-dee-dee-dee" call. Also gives a high-pitched, two-toned "fee-bee" call. Can have different calls in different regions.

Mountain Chickadee
Poecile gambeli

YEAR-ROUND

Size: 5½" (14 cm)

Male: Gray overall with a black cap, chin, and line through the eyes. White eyebrows.

Female: same as male

Juvenile: similar to adult

Nest: cavity, old woodpecker hole or excavates its own, or uses a nest box; female builds; 1–2 broods per year

Eggs: 5–8; white without markings

Incubation: 11–14 days; female incubates

Fledging: 18–21 days; female and male feed the young

Migration: non-migrator to partial migrator

Food: seeds, insects; visits seed and suet feeders

Compare: The Black-capped Chickadee (p. 227) is similar, but it lacks the white eyebrows of the Mountain Chickadee. Larger than Bushtit (p. 223), which lacks the black cap and white on face.

Stan's Notes: An abundant bird in the state, but more common in coniferous forests in mountainous regions of Nevada. Preferring old growth spruce, fir, and pine forests, it feeds heavily on coniferous seeds and insects. Usually will not mingle with Black-capped Chickadees, but does flock with other birds during winter. Moves to lower elevations in winter, returning to high elevations for nesting. Excavates a nest cavity or uses an old woodpecker hole. Will use a nest box. Occasionally uses the same nest site year after year. Lines its nest with moss, hair, and feathers. Female will not leave her nest if disturbed, but will hiss and flutter wings.

female
p. 103

male

gray-headed

Oregon
male

Dark-eyed Junco
Junco hyemalis

YEAR-ROUND
WINTER

Size: 5½" (14 cm)

Male: Plump, dark-eyed bird with a slate-gray-to-charcoal chest, head, and back. White belly. Pink bill. White outer tail feathers appear like a white V in flight.

Female: round with brown plumage

Juvenile: similar to female, with streaking on the breast and head

Nest: cup on the ground; female builds; 2 broods per year

Eggs: 3–5; white with reddish-brown markings

Incubation: 12–13 days; female incubates

Fledging: 10–13 days; male and female feed the young

Migration: partial migrator to non-migrator in Nevada

Food: seeds, insects; visits ground and seed feeders

Compare: Rarely confused with any other bird. Look for the pink bill and small flocks feeding under feeders to identify the male Dark-eyed Junco.

Stan's Notes: One of the most numerous birds in the state. Common year-round bird of Nevada, spending winters in foothills and plains after snowmelt, returning to higher elevations for nesting. Adheres to a rigid social hierarchy, with dominant birds chasing the less dominant birds. Look for the white outer tail feathers flashing in flight. Often seen in small flocks on the ground, where it uses its feet to simultaneously "double-scratch" to expose seeds and insects. Eats many weed seeds. Nests in a wide variety of wooded habitats in April and May. Several subspecies of Dark-eyed Junco were previously considered to be separate species (see lower insets).

male

female

YEAR-ROUND

White-breasted Nuthatch
Sitta carolinensis

Size: 5–6" (13–15 cm)

Male: Slate gray with a white face, breast, and belly. Large white patch on the rump. Black cap and nape. Bill is long and thin, slightly upturned. Chestnut undertail.

Female: similar to male, but has a gray cap and nape

Juvenile: similar to female

Nest: cavity; female builds a nest within; 1 brood per year

Eggs: 5–7; white with brown markings

Incubation: 11–12 days; female incubates

Fledging: 13–14 days; female and male feed the young

Migration: non-migrator

Food: insects, insect eggs, seeds; comes to seed and suet feeders

Compare: Red-breasted Nuthatch (p. 221) is smaller and has a rust-red belly and distinctive black eye line.

Stan's Notes: The nuthatch hops headfirst down trees, looking for insects missed by birds climbing up. Its climbing agility is due to an extra-long hind toe claw, or nail, that is nearly twice the size of its front claws. "Nuthatch," from the Middle English *nuthak*, refers to the bird's habit of wedging a seed in a crevice and hacking it open. Often seen in flocks with Brown Creepers, chickadees, and Downy Woodpeckers. Mates stay together year-round, defending a small territory. Gives a characteristic "whi-whi-whi-whi" spring call during February through May. One of nearly 30 worldwide nuthatch species.

male

female

Yellow-rumped Warbler
Setophaga coronata

YEAR-ROUND
SUMMER
MIGRATION
WINTER

Size: 5–6" (13–15 cm)

Male: Slate gray with black streaking on the chest. Yellow patches on the head, flanks, and rump. White chin and belly. Two white wing bars.

Female: duller gray than the male, mixed with brown

Juvenile: first winter is similar to the adult female

Nest: cup; female builds; 2 broods per year

Eggs: 4–5; white with brown markings

Incubation: 12–13 days; female incubates

Fledging: 10–12 days; female and male feed young

Migration: complete, to Arizona, New Mexico, Mexico and Central America; non-migrator in parts of Nevada

Food: insects, berries; visits suet feeders in spring

Compare: The male Common Yellowthroat (p. 327) has a yellow chest and distinctive black mask. Look for patches of yellow on the rump, head, flanks, and chin of Yellow-rumped Warbler to help identify.

Stan's Notes: A common warbler in Nevada, nesting in coniferous and aspen forests. Flocks of hundreds seen during migration. Familiar call is a single robust "chip," heard mostly during migration. Sings a wonderful song in spring. Moves quickly among trees and from the ground to trees. Flits around the upper branches of tall trees. In the fall, the male molts to a dull color similar to the female, but he retains his yellow patches all year. The subspecies in eastern states is known as the Myrtle Warbler; the western subspecies is known as the Audubon's Warbler. Sometimes called Butter-butt due to the yellow patch on its rump.

YEAR-ROUND

Juniper Titmouse
Baeolophus ridgwayi

Size: 6" (15 cm)

Male: All gray with a crest. Dark eyes. Small gray bill. Upper wings may have faint brown tinge.

Female: same as male

Juvenile: similar to adult, often lighter in color, lacks a well-developed crest

Nest: cavity; female builds; 1 brood per year

Eggs: 3–6; white without markings

Incubation: 14–16 days; female incubates

Fledging: 16–21 days; female and male feed young

Migration: non-migrator; moves around to find food

Food: seeds, insects, fruit; comes to seed and suet feeders

Compare: Mountain Chickadee (p. 229) is slightly smaller, has a black cap and lacks a crest. Verdin (p. 225) is smaller, has a yellow head and lacks a crest.

Stan's Notes: A very drab-looking bird usually found in open dry habitats. Can be attracted to your yard with a nest box. The female does not usually fly when approached at the nest, but will fluff up and hiss to protect her eggs. Like the chickadee, it builds a similar nest with green moss and grass and lines it with animal fur. Mated pairs often remain together throughout the season. This species was once considered the same as the Oak Titmouse (*B. inornatus*).

Say's Phoebe

Sayornis saya

YEAR-ROUND
SUMMER

Size:	7½" (19 cm)
Male:	Overall dark gray, darkest on head, tail, and wings. Belly and undertail tawny. Black bill.
Female:	same as male
Juvenile:	similar to adult, but browner overall with 2 tawny wing bars and a yellow lower bill
Nest:	cup; female builds; 1–2 broods per year
Eggs:	3–6; pale white with brown markings
Incubation:	12–14 days; female incubates
Fledging:	14–16 days; female and male feed young
Migration:	complete, to Arizona, New Mexico, Mexico, and Central America; non-migrator in parts of Nevada
Food:	insects, berries
Compare:	Smaller than Western Kingbird (p. 343), which has a yellow belly, not the tawny belly of Say's Phoebe.

Stan's Notes: A widespread bird in Nevada below 9,000-foot (2,750 m) elevations. Nests in cliff crevices, abandoned buildings, bridges, and other vertical structures. Frequently uses the same nest a couple of times in a season, returning the following year to that same nest. Has a nearly all-insect diet. Flies out from a perch to grab an aerial insect and returns to the same perch (hawking). Also hunts insects on the ground, hovering and dropping down to catch them. Phoebes are classified as New World Flycatchers and aren't related to Old World Flycatchers. Named after Thomas Say, who is said to have first recorded this bird in Colorado. The genus, species, and first part of its common name refer to Mr. Say. Common name "Phoebe" is likely an imitation of the bird's call.

American Dipper
Cinclus mexicanus

YEAR-ROUND

Size: 7½" (19 cm)

Male: Dark gray to black overall. Head is slightly lighter in color. Short upturned tail. Dark eyes and bill.

Female: same as male

Juvenile: similar to adult, only paler with white eyelids that are most noticeable when blinking

Nest: pendulous, covered nest with the entrance near the bottom, on cliff, behind waterfall; female builds; 1–2 broods per year

Eggs: 3–5; white without markings

Incubation: 13–17 days; female incubates

Fledging: 18–25 days; female and male feed young

Migration: non-migrator; seeks moving open water

Food: aquatic insects, small fish, crustaceans

Compare: American Robin (p. 251) is a similar shape, but it has a red breast. The only songbird in the state that dives into fast-moving water.

Stan's Notes: A common bird of fast, usually noisy streams that provide some kind of protected shelf on which to construct a nest. Some have had success attracting with man-made ledges. Plunges headfirst into fast-moving water, looking for just about any aquatic insect, propelling itself underwater with its wings. Frequently seen emerging with a large insect, which it smashes against rock before eating. Has the ability to fly directly into the air from underwater. Depending on snowmelt, nesting usually starts in March or April. American Dippers in lower elevations often nest for a second time each season.

Sage Thrasher

Oreoscoptes montanus

SUMMER MIGRATION

Size: 8½" (22 cm)

Male: Light gray overall with a heavily streaked white chest. Distinctive white chin. Yellow-orange eyes. Darker gray tail with white tip.

Female: same as male

Juvenile: duller version of adult

Nest: cup; the female and male build; 1–2 broods per year

Eggs: 3–5; blue with brown markings

Incubation: 13–17 days; female and male incubate

Fledging: 11–14 days; female and male feed young

Migration: complete, to Arizona, New Mexico, Mexico, and Central America

Food: insects, fruit

Compare: Townsend's Solitaire (p. 245) is the same size, but lacks a streaked breast. Northern Mockingbird (p. 253) is larger and has a clear chest and obvious white wing patches, seen in flight.

Stan's Notes: Common in the sagebrush regions of Nevada. Sagebrush regions are known for unique birdlife. Males are often seen and heard as they sing from the tops of shrubs. Will construct a large and bulky nest at the base of a tree or beneath dense cover in an attempt to keep the nest shaded. Sometimes constructs a twig platform over nest if existing cover doesn't provide enough shade. Old nests are sometimes used by Gambel's Quails. Returns in April. Nesting in May.

YEAR-ROUND
WINTER

Townsend's Solitaire
Myadestes townsendi

Size: 8½" (22 cm)

Male: All-gray robin look-alike. Prominent white ring around each eye. Wings slightly darker than the body. Long tail. Short dark bill. Dark legs.

Female: same as male

Juvenile: darker gray with a tan, scaly appearance

Nest: cup; female builds; 1–2 broods per year

Eggs: 3–5; blue, green, gray, or white with brown markings

Incubation: 12–14 days; female incubates

Fledging: 10–14 days; female and male feed young

Migration: non-migrator to partial, to the Southwest and Mexico; known to migrate to eastern states

Food: insects, fruit

Compare: American Robin (p. 251) has a red breast. The Northern Mockingbird (p. 251) lacks the white eye-ring. Clark's Nutcracker (p. 259) has black wings.

Stan's Notes: A summer resident of coniferous mountain forests, moving lower in winter. "Hawks" for insects, perching in trees and darting out to capture them. Eats berries in winter when insects are not available and actively defends a good berry source from other birds. Builds nest on ground sheltered by rocks or an over-hang, or sometimes low in a tree or shrub. Song is a series of clear flute-like whistles without a distinct pattern. Shows white outer tail feathers and light-tan patches on wings when in flight.

gray morph

brown morph

Western Screech-Owl

Megascops kennicottii

YEAR-ROUND

Size: 8–9" (20–23 cm); up to 1¾' wingspan

Male: A small, overall gray owl with bright-yellow eyes. Two short ear tufts. A short tail. Some birds are brownish.

Female: same as male

Juvenile: similar to adult of the same morph and lacks ear tufts

Nest: cavity, old woodpecker hole; 1 brood per year

Eggs: 2–6; white without markings

Incubation: 21–30 days; female incubates

Fledging: 25–30 days; male and female feed the young

Migration: non-migrator

Food: large insects, small mammals, birds

Compare: Burrowing Owl (p. 143) is slightly larger and lacks ear tufts. Western Screech-Owl is hard to confuse with its considerably larger cousin, Great Horned Owl (p. 203).

Stan's Notes: This is the most common small owl throughout Nevada. An owl of suburban woodlands and backyards. Requires trees that are at least a foot in diameter for nesting and roosting, so it usually is found in towns or in trees that have been preserved. A secondary cavity nester, which means it nests in tree cavities created by other birds. Usually not found in elevations above 4,000 feet (1,200 m). Densities in areas with lower elevations are about 1 bird per square mile (2.5 sq. km). Most screech-owls are gray; some are brown (see inset).

Loggerhead Shrike
Lanius ludovicianus

YEAR-ROUND
MIGRATION

Size: 9" (22.5 cm)

Male: Gray head and back and a white chin, breast, and belly. Black wings, tail, legs, and feet. Black mask across the eyes and a black bill with a hooked tip. White wing patches, seen in flight.

Female: same as male

Juvenile: dull version of adult

Nest: cup; male and female construct; 1–2 broods per year

Eggs: 4–7; off-white with dark markings

Incubation: 16–17 days; female incubates

Fledging: 17–21 days; female and male feed the young

Migration: non-migrator to partial in Nevada

Food: insects, lizards, small mammals, frogs

Compare: The Northern Mockingbird (p. 253) has a similar color pattern, but it lacks the black mask. The Cedar Waxwing (p. 131) has a black mask, but it is a brown bird, not gray and black like the Loggerhead Shrike.

Stan's Notes: The Loggerhead is a songbird that acts like a bird of prey. Known for skewering prey on barbed wire fences, thorns, and other sharp objects to store or hold still while tearing apart to eat, hence its other common name, Butcher Bird. Feet are too weak to hold the prey it eats. Breeding bird surveys indicate declining populations in the Great Plains due to pesticides killing its major food source—grasshoppers.

male

female

American Robin
Turdus migratorius

YEAR-ROUND

Size: 9–11" (23–28 cm)

Male: Familiar gray bird with a dark rust-red breast and a nearly black head and tail. White chin with black streaks. White eye-ring.

Female: similar to male, with a duller rust-red breast and a gray head

Juvenile: similar to female, with a speckled breast and brown back

Nest: cup; female builds with help from the male; 2–3 broods per year

Eggs: 4–7; pale blue without markings

Incubation: 12–14 days; female incubates

Fledging: 14–16 days; female and male feed the young

Migration: non-migrator; birds from northern states increase population during winter

Food: insects, fruit, berries, earthworms

Compare: Familiar bird to all. To differentiate the male from the female, compare the nearly black head and rust-red chest of the male with the gray head and duller chest of the female.

Stan's Notes: Although complete migrators, they can be seen year-round in most of the state. Can be heard singing all night long in spring. City robins sing louder than country robins in order to hear one another over traffic and noise. A robin isn't listening for worms when it turns its head to one side. It is focusing its sight out of one eye to look for dirt moving, which is caused by worms moving. Territorial, often fighting its reflection in a window.

displaying

Northern Mockingbird
Mimus polyglottos

YEAR-ROUND

Size: 10" (25 cm)

Male: Silvery-gray head and back with a light-gray breast and belly. White wing patches, seen in flight or during display. Tail mostly black with white outer tail feathers. Black bill.

Female: same as male

Juvenile: dull gray with a heavily streaked breast and a gray bill

Nest: cup; female and male construct; 2 broods per year, sometimes more

Eggs: 3–5; blue-green with brown markings

Incubation: 12–13 days; female incubates

Fledging: 11–13 days; female and male feed the young

Migration: partial migrator to non-migrator in Nevada

Food: insects, fruit

Compare: Loggerhead Shrike (p. 249) has a similar color pattern, but it is stockier, has a black mask, and perches in more-open places. Townsend's Solitaire (p. 245) has a white eye-ring. Look for Mockingbird to spread its wings, flash its white wing patches, and wag its tail from side to side.

Stan's Notes: A very animated bird. Performs an elaborate mating dance. Facing each other with heads and tails erect, pairs will run toward each other, flashing their white wing patches, and then retreat to cover nearby. Thought to flash the wing patches to scare up insects when hunting. Sits for long periods on top of shrubs. Imitates other birds (vocal mimicry); hence the common name. Young males often sing at night. Often unafraid of people, allowing for close observation.

male

female

California Quail
Callipepla californica

YEAR-ROUND

Size: 10" (25 cm)

Male: Plump gray quail with black face and chin. Prominent teardrop-shaped plume on the forehead. "Scaled" appearance on the belly, light brown to white. Pale-brown forehead.

Female: similar to male, lacks a black face and chin, and has a shorter plume

Juvenile: similar to female

Nest: ground; female builds; 1 brood per year

Eggs: 12–16; white with brown markings

Incubation: 18–23 days; female incubates

Fledging: 8–10 days; female and male teach young to feed

Migration: non-migrator

Food: seeds, leaves, insects; visits ground feeders

Compare: Male Gambel's Quail (p. 257) is the same size with a rusty-red crest and dark patch on the belly. Ring-necked Pheasant (p. 211) is larger and lacks the unique plume on the head of the Quail.

Stan's Notes: Prefers open fields, agricultural areas and sagebrush. Not found in dense forests or at high elevations. Rarely flies, preferring to run away. Roosts in trees or dense shrubs at night, not on the ground. Usually seen in groups (coveys) of up to 100 individuals during winter, breaking up into small family units for breeding. Young stay with the family group until autumn.

male

female

YEAR-ROUND

Gambel's Quail
Callipepla gambelii

Size: 10" (25 cm)

Male: A plump round bird with a short tail. Gray chest, back, and tail. Rusty crest outlined in white. Dark chin, throat, and forehead with a unique dark plume emanating from the forehead. Rusty sides with white streaks. A dark patch on belly. Black bill. Gray legs.

Female: similar to male, lacks a rusty crest and dark chin, throat, and forehead, plume less robust

Juvenile: similar to female

Nest: ground; female builds; 1–2 broods per year

Eggs: 8–12; dull white with brown markings

Incubation: 21–24 days; female incubates

Fledging: 7–10 days; female and male show the young what to eat

Migration: non-migrator

Food: seeds, leaves, insects, fruit; comes to seed feeders on the ground

Compare: Smaller than Chukar (p. 265). Look for Gambel's unique plume to help identify.

Stan's Notes: A native species. Prefers arid scrubby regions with a constant water source. Winter flocks of up to 20 birds (coveys) split up during breeding season. Covey walks in single file. Able to hop on and over fences. Scurries across open areas to reach cover. Visits feeders in early morning and late afternoon. Takes dust baths in dirt depressions, kicking dust over body to get rid of small insects. Builds cup nest under vegetation, lining it with grass and feathers. Male gives a distinctive, repetitious call, "yup-waay-yup-yup."

Clark's Nutcracker
Nucifraga columbiana

YEAR-ROUND

Size: 12" (30 cm)

Male: Gray with black wings and a narrow black band down the center of tail. Small white patches on long wings, seen in flight. Has a relatively short tail with a white undertail.

Female: same as male

Juvenile: same as adult

Nest: cup; female and male build; 1 brood a year

Eggs: 2–5; pale green with brown markings

Incubation: 16–18 days; female and male incubate

Fledging: 18–21 days; male and female feed young

Migration: non-migrator

Food: seeds, insects, berries, eggs, mammals

Compare: Townsend's Solitaire (p. 245) is smaller, lacks black wings, and has a smaller bill. The Steller's Jay (p. 87) is dark blue with a black crest. Look for the Nutcracker's black wings.

Stan's Notes: A high-country bird found in coniferous forests in Nevada. It has a varied diet but relies heavily on piñon seeds, frequently caching large amounts to consume later or feed to young. Has a large pouch under its tongue (sublingual pouch), which it uses to transport seeds. Studies show the birds can carry up to 100 seeds at a time. Nests early in the year, often while snow still covers the ground, relying on stored foods. A "Lewis and Clark" bird, first recorded by William Clark in 1805 in Idaho.

YEAR-ROUND

Eurasian Collared-Dove
Streptopelia decaocto

Size: 12½" (32 cm)

Male: Head, neck, breast, and belly are gray to tan. Back, wings, and tail are slightly darker. Thin black collar with a white border on the nape of the neck. Tail is long and squared.

Female: same as male

Juvenile: similar to adults

Nest: platform; female and male build; 2–3 broods per year

Eggs: 1–2; creamy white without markings

Incubation: 14–18 days; female and male incubate

Fledging: 15–20 days; female and male feed the young

Migration: non-migrator

Food: seeds; will visit ground and seed feeders

Compare: The Mourning Dove (p. 153) is slightly smaller and darker. The Rock Pigeon (p. 263) has colorful iridescent patches. Look for the black collar on the nape and the squared tail to help identify the Eurasian Collared-Dove.

Stan's Notes: This non-native bird has spread into Nevada, having moved into Florida in the early 1980s after inadvertent introduction to the Bahamas. It has been expanding its range across North America and is predicted to spread just like it did through Europe from Asia. Nearly identical to the Ringed Turtle-Dove, a common pet bird. The dark mark on the back of the neck gave rise to the common name. Look for flashes of white in the tail and dark wing tips when it lands or takes off.

Rock Pigeon
Columba livia

YEAR-ROUND

Size: 13" (33 cm)

Male: No set color pattern. Shades of gray to white with patches of gleaming, iridescent green and blue. Often has a light rump patch.

Female: same as male

Juvenile: same as adults

Nest: platform; female builds; 3–4 broods per year

Eggs: 1–2; white without markings

Incubation: 18–20 days; female and male incubate

Fledging: 25–26 days; female and male feed the young

Migration: non-migrator

Food: seeds

Compare: The Eurasian Collared-Dove (p. 261) has a black collar on the nape. The Mourning Dove (p. 153) is smaller and light brown and lacks the variety of color combinations of the Rock Pigeon.

Stan's Notes: Also known as the Domestic Pigeon. Formerly known as the Rock Dove. Introduced to North America from Europe by the early settlers. Most common around cities and barnyards, where it scratches for seeds. One of the few birds with a wide variety of colors, produced by years of selective breeding while in captivity. Parents feed the young a regurgitated liquid known as crop-milk for the first few days of life. One of the few birds that can drink without tilting its head back. Nests under bridges or on buildings, balconies, barns, and sheds. Was once thought to be a nuisance in cities and was poisoned. Now, many cities have Peregrine Falcons (p. 273) feeding on Rock Pigeons, which keeps their numbers in check.

Chukar
Alectoris chukar

YEAR-ROUND

Size: 14" (36 cm)

Male: Plump round bird with a short tail. Overall gray with a cream-colored throat. Black line runs through the eyes and down the neck to breast, outlining the throat. Bold dark hash marks on sides. Buffy orange under the tail. Small reddish orange bill and orange legs.

Female: same as male

Juvenile: similar to adult

Nest: ground; female builds; 1 brood per year

Eggs: 7–15; yellow to white with brown markings

Incubation: 22–24 days; female incubates

Fledging: 7–10 days; female and male show the young what to eat

Migration: non-migrator

Food: seeds, insects, leaves, fruit

Compare: Gambel's Quail (p. 257) is smaller and has a plume on forehead and a black throat.

Stan's Notes: This non-native species was introduced into many parts of North America from Eurasia. A game bird inadvertently released by hunters who train hunting dogs. Year-round resident in arid regions that support healthy grass, which produces heavy seed crops. Often in flocks of up to 20 birds (coveys), usually family members, in winter. Roosts at night in tight circles on the ground, tails together, heads pointing out to watch for predators. Builds a well-concealed cup nest amid rocks or in a shallow depression. Lines nest with dried grass and feathers. "Chukar" comes from its call, which is given to gather family members or attract a mate.

breeding
p. 157

displaying

winter

Willet

Tringa semipalmata

SUMMER MIGRATION

Size: 14–16" (36–40 cm)

Male: Winter plumage is gray with a white belly. A distinctive black-and-white wing lining pattern, seen in flight or during display. Gray bill and legs.

Female: same as male

Juvenile: similar to breeding adult, more tan in color

Nest: ground; female and male build; 1 brood per year

Eggs: 3–5; olive-green with dark markings

Incubation: 24–28 days; male and female incubate

Fledging: 1–2 days; female and male feed young

Migration: complete, to parts of California, the coast of Mexico, and Central and South America

Food: insects, small fish, crabs, worms, clams

Compare: Larger than Spotted Sandpiper (p. 133). Killdeer (p. 149) has 2 black neck bands. Look for the long dark legs of the Willet.

Stan's Notes: Northern birds pass through coastal California to destinations farther south. It appears a rich, warm brown during the breeding season and rather plain gray during the winter, but it always has a striking black-and-white wing pattern when seen in flight. Uses its black-and-white wing patches to display to its mate. Named after the "pill-will-willet" call it gives during the breeding season. Gives a "kip-kip-kip" alarm call when it takes flight. It nests in northern Nevada, other western states, along the East Coast and in Canada.

soaring

juvenile

Sharp-shinned Hawk

Accipiter striatus

YEAR-ROUND
WINTER

Size: 10–14" (25–36 cm); up to 2' wingspan

Male: Small woodland hawk with a gray back and head and a rust-red chest. Short wings. Long, squared tail and several dark tail bands, with the widest at the end of the tail. Red eyes.

Female: same as male but larger

Juvenile: same size as adults, with a brown back, heavy streaking on the chest, and yellow eyes

Nest: platform; female builds; 1 brood per year

Eggs: 4–5; white with brown markings

Incubation: 32–35 days; female incubates

Fledging: 24–27 days; female and male feed the young

Migration: complete migrator, to southwestern states, Mexico, and Central America; non-migrator in much of Nevada

Food: birds, small mammals

Compare: Cooper's Hawk (p. 271) is larger and has a larger head, a slightly longer neck, and a rounded tail. Look for the squared tail to help identify the Sharp-shinned Hawk.

Stan's Notes: A hawk of backyards, parks, and woodlands. Seen swooping on birds visiting feeders and chasing them as they flee. Its short wingspan and long tail help it to maneuver through thick stands of trees in pursuit of prey. Calls a loud, high-pitched "kik-kik-kik-kik." Named "Sharp-shinned" for the sharp projection (keel) on the leading edge of its shin. A bird's shin is actually below the ankle (rather than above it, like ours) on the tarsus bone of its foot. In most birds, the tarsus bone is rounded, not sharp.

soaring

juvenile

Cooper's Hawk
Accipiter cooperii

YEAR-ROUND

Size: 14–20" (36–51 cm); up to 3' wingspan

Male: Medium-size hawk with short wings and a long, rounded tail with several black bands. Slate-gray back, rusty breast, dark wing tips. Gray bill with a bright-yellow spot at the base. Dark-red eyes.

Female: similar to male but larger

Juvenile: brown back, brown streaking on the breast, bright-yellow eyes

Nest: platform; male and female construct; 1 brood per year

Eggs: 2–4; bluish white without markings

Incubation: 32–36 days; female and male incubate

Fledging: 28–32 days; male and female feed the young

Migration: non-migrator to partial migrator; will move around to find food

Food: small birds, mammals

Compare: Sharp-shinned Hawk (p. 269) is much smaller, lighter gray and has a squared tail. Look for the banded, rounded tail to help identify Cooper's Hawk.

Stan's Notes: Found in many habitats, from woodlands to parks and backyards. Stubby wings help it to navigate around trees while it chases small birds. Will ambush prey, flying into heavy brush or even running on the ground. Comes to feeders, hunting for birds. Flies with long glides followed by a few quick flaps. Calls a loud, clear "cack-cack-cack-cack." The young have gray eyes that turn bright yellow at 1 year and turn dark red later, after 3–5 years.

juvenile

in-flight juvenile

in flight

Peregrine Falcon
Falco peregrinus

YEAR-ROUND

Size: 16–20" (41–51 cm); up to 3¾' wingspan

Male: Dark-gray back and tan-to-white chest. Horizontal bars on belly, legs, and undertail. Dark "hood" head marking and wide black mustache. Yellow base of bill and eye-ring. Yellow legs.

Female: similar to male but noticeably larger

Juvenile: overall darker than adults, with heavy streaking on the chest and belly

Nest: ground (scrape) on a cliff edge, tall building, bridge, or smokestack; 1 brood per year

Eggs: 3–4; white, some with brown markings

Incubation: 29–32 days; female and male incubate

Fledging: 35–42 days; male and female feed the young

Migration: non-migrator in Nevada

Food: birds (Rock Pigeons in cities; shorebirds and waterfowl in rural areas)

Compare: The American Kestrel (p. 145) is smaller and has 2 vertical black stripes on its face. Look for the dark "hood" head marking and mustache marks to identify the Peregrine Falcon.

Stan's Notes: A wide-bodied raptor that hunts many bird species. The larger females hunt larger prey. Lives in many cities, diving (stooping) on pigeons at speeds of up to 200 miles (322 km) per hour, which knocks them to the ground. Soars with its wings flat, often riding thermals. During courtship, the male brings food to the female and performs aerial displays. Likes to nest on a high ledge or platform for a good view of its territory. A solitary nester and monogamous.

female
p. 193

male

soaring

Northern Harrier
Circus hudsonius

YEAR-ROUND
WINTER

Size: 18–22" (45–56 cm); up to 4' wingspan

Male: Slender, low-flying hawk. Silver-gray with a large white rump patch and white belly. Long tail with faint narrow bands. Black wing tips. Yellow eyes.

Female: dark-brown back, brown streaking on breast and belly, large white rump patch, thin black tail bands, black wing tips, yellow eyes

Juvenile: similar to female, with an orange breast

Nest: ground; female and male construct; 1 brood per year

Eggs: 4–8; bluish white without markings

Incubation: 31–32 days; female incubates

Fledging: 30–35 days; male and female feed the young

Migration: partial migrator, to southwestern states, Mexico, and Central America; non-migrator in much of Nevada

Food: mice, snakes, insects, small birds

Compare: Slimmer than the Red-tailed Hawk (p. 199). Cooper's Hawk (p. 271) has a rusty breast. Look for a low-gliding hawk with a large white rump patch to identify the male Harrier.

Stan's Notes: One of the easiest of hawks to identify. Glides just above the ground, following the contours of the land while searching for prey. Holds its wings just above horizontal, tilting back and forth in the wind, similar to Turkey Vultures. Formerly called the Marsh Hawk due to its habit of hunting over marshes. Feeds and nests on the ground. Will also preen and rest on the ground. Unlike other hawks, mainly uses its hearing to find prey, followed by sight. At any age, has a distinctive owl-like face disk.

female
p. 185

male

Gadwall
Mareca strepera

YEAR-ROUND
SUMMER
WINTER

Size: 19" (48 cm)

Male: A plump gray duck with a brown head and a distinctive black rump. White belly. Chestnut-tinged wings. Bright-white wing linings. Small white wing patch, seen when swimming. Gray bill.

Female: similar to female Mallard, a mottled brown with a pronounced color change from dark-brown body to light-brown neck and head, bright-white wing linings, small white wing patch, gray bill with orange sides

Juvenile: similar to female

Nest: ground; female lines the nest with fine grass and down feathers plucked from her chest; 1 brood per year

Eggs: 8–11; white without markings

Incubation: 24–27 days; female incubates

Fledging: 48–56 days; young feed themselves

Migration: complete, to southwestern states, Mexico; a few remain in winter in Nevada

Food: aquatic insects and plants

Compare: Male Gadwall is one of the few gray ducks. Look for its distinctive black rump.

Stan's Notes: A duck of shallow marshes. Consumes mostly plant material, dunking its head in water to feed rather than tipping forward, like other dabbling ducks. Most commonly seen during spring and fall migrations. Frequently in pairs with other duck species. Nests within 300 feet (90 m) of water. Establishes pair bond in winter.

in flight

Canada Goose

Branta canadensis

YEAR-ROUND WINTER

Size: 25–43" (64–109 cm); up to 5½' wingspan

Male: Large gray goose with a black neck and head. White chin and cheek strap.

Female: same as male

Juvenile: same as adults

Nest: platform, on the ground; female builds; 1 brood per year

Eggs: 5–10; white without markings

Incubation: 25–30 days; female incubates

Fledging: 42–55 days; male and female teach the young to feed

Migration: non-migrator to partial in Nevada

Food: aquatic plants, insects, seeds

Compare: Large goose that is rarely confused with any other bird.

Stan's Notes: Common year-round residents in the state, breeding throughout northern Nevada. Flocks fly in a large V when traveling long distances. Begins breeding in the third year. Adults mate for many years. If threatened, they will hiss as a warning. Males stand as sentinels at the edge of their group and will bob their heads and become aggressive if approached. Adults molt their primary flight feathers while raising their young, rendering family groups temporarily flightless. Several subspecies vary in the US. Generally eastern groups are paler than western. Their size also varies, decreasing northward. The smallest subspecies is in the Arctic.

in flight

YEAR-ROUND
MIGRATION

Great Blue Heron
Ardea herodias

Size: 42–48" (107–122 cm); up to 6' wingspan

Male: Tall and gray. Black eyebrows end in long plumes at the back of the head. Long yellow bill. Long feathers at the base of the neck drop down in a kind of necklace. Long legs.

Female: same as male

Juvenile: same as adults, but more brown than gray, with a black crown; lacks plumes

Nest: platform in a colony; male and female build; 1 brood per year

Eggs: 3–5; pale blue without markings

Incubation: 27–28 days; female and male incubate

Fledging: 56–60 days; male and female feed the young

Migration: non-migrator; will move around to find food in winter

Food: small fish, frogs, insects, snakes, baby birds

Compare: The Sandhill Crane (p. 283) has a red cap. Look for the long, yellow bill to help identify the Great Blue Heron.

Stan's Notes: One of the most common herons. Found in open water, from small ponds to large lakes. Stalks small fish in shallow water. Will strike at mice, squirrels, and nearly anything it comes across. Red-winged Blackbirds will attack it to stop it from taking their babies out of the nest. In flight, it holds its neck in an S shape and slightly cups its wings, while the legs trail straight out behind. Nests in a colony of up to 100 birds. Nests in trees near or hanging over water. Barks like a dog when startled.

in flight

rusty
stain

in-flight
rusty stain

Sandhill Crane

Antigone canadensis

SUMMER
MIGRATION

Size: 42–48" (107–122 cm); up to 7' wingspan

Male: Elegant gray crane with long legs and neck. Wings and body often rust brown from mud staining. Scarlet-red cap. Yellow to red eyes.

Female: same as male

Juvenile: dull brown with yellow eyes; lacks a red cap

Nest: ground; female and male construct; 1 brood per year

Eggs: 2; olive with brown markings

Incubation: 28–32 days; female and male incubate

Fledging: 65 days; female and male feed the young

Migration: complete, to Arizona, New Mexico, and Mexico

Food: insects, fruit, worms, plants, amphibians

Compare: Great Blue Heron (p. 281) has a longer bill and holds its neck in an S shape during flight. Look for the scarlet-red cap to help identify the Sandhill Crane.

Stan's Notes: Preens mud into its feathers, staining its plumage rust brown (see insets). Gives a very loud and distinctive rattling call, often heard before the bird is seen. Flight is characteristic, with a faster upstroke, making the wings look like they're flicking in flight. Can fly at heights of over 10,000 feet (3,050 m). Nests on the ground in a large mound of aquatic vegetation. Performs a spectacular mating dance: The birds will face each other, then bow and jump into the air while making loud cackling sounds and flapping their wings. They will also flip sticks and grass into the air during their dance.

male

female

Calliope Hummingbird

Selasphorus calliope

SUMMER

Size: 3¼" (8 cm)

Male: Iridescent green head, back, and tail. Breast and belly white to tan. V-shaped iridescent rosy red throat patch (gorget). A very short, thin bill and short tail compared with other hummingbirds. Wing tips reach to tip of tail.

Female: same as male, but thin, spotty throat patch

Juvenile: similar to female

Nest: cup; female builds; 1 brood per year

Eggs: 1–2; white without markings

Incubation: 15–17 days; female incubates

Fledging: 18–22 days; female feeds the young

Migration: complete, to Central and South America

Food: nectar, insects; will come to nectar feeders

Compare: Smaller than other hummingbirds. Look for a short thin bill, short tail and wing tips extending past the tail when perched. Male Broad-tailed (p. 289) is very similar with a slightly longer tail.

Stan's Notes: The smallest bird in North America. Common in open forest and brushy areas in lower elevations. A relatively quiet bird that will come to nectar feeders. During the breeding season, males can be heard zinging around while displaying for females. Females are hard to distinguish from other female hummingbirds. Often builds nest on branches of pine trees. Juvenile males obtain a partial throat patch by fall of their first year.

male

female

Black-chinned Hummingbird

Archilochus alexandri

SUMMER
MIGRATION

Size: 3¾" (9.5 cm)

Male: Tiny iridescent green bird with black throat patch (gorget) that reflects violet-blue in sunlight. Black chin. White chest and belly.

Female: same as male, but lacking the throat patch and black chin, has white flanks

Juvenile: similar to female

Nest: cup; female builds; 1–2 broods per year

Eggs: 1–3; white without markings

Incubation: 13–16 days; female incubates

Fledging: 19–21 days; female feeds young

Migration: complete, to Central and South America

Food: nectar, insects; will come to nectar feeders

Compare: Male Broad-tailed Hummingbird (p. 289) is slightly larger and has a rosy-red throat patch and lacks a black chin. The flanks of female Broad-tailed (p. 289) are tan, not white, like female Black-chinned's.

Stan's Notes: One of the smallest birds in Nevada and one of several hummingbird species in the state, these are the only birds with the ability to fly backward. Doesn't sing. Will chatter or buzz to communicate. Wings create a humming noise, flapping nearly 80 times per second. Weighing only 2–3 grams, it takes approximately five average-sized hummingbirds to equal the weight of one chickadee. Males return first at the end of April. Male performs a spectacular pendulum-like flight over a perched female. After mating, the female builds a nest, using spiderwebs to glue nest materials together, and raises young without the mate's help. More than one clutch per year not uncommon.

287

male

female

SUMMER
MIGRATION

Broad-tailed Hummingbird

Selasphorus platycercus

Size: 4" (10 cm)

Male: Tiny iridescent green bird with a black throat patch (gorget) that reflects rosy red in sunlight. Wings and part of the back are green. White chest.

Female: same as male, but lacking the throat patch, much more green on back, tan flanks

Juvenile: similar to female

Nest: cup; female builds; 1–2 broods per year

Eggs: 1–3; white without markings

Incubation: 16–19 days; female incubates

Fledging: 20–22 days; female feeds young

Migration: complete, to Central and South America

Food: nectar, insects; will come to nectar feeders

Compare: The male Black-chinned Hummingbird (p. 287) is slightly smaller and has a violet-blue throat patch and a black chin. Female Black-chinned (p. 287) has white flanks, unlike the tan flanks of female Broad-tailed.

Stan's Notes: Hummingbirds are the only birds with the ability to fly backward. Does not sing. Will chatter or buzz to communicate. Wingbeats produce a whistle, almost like a tiny ringing bell. Heart pumps up to an incredible 1,260 beats every minute. Weighing just 2–3 grams, it takes about five average-sized hummingbirds to equal the weight of one chickadee. Male performs a spectacular pendulum-like flight over the perched female. After mating, female builds the nest and raises young without any help from her mate. Constructs a soft, flexible nest that expands to accommodate the growing young.

male

female

Violet-green Swallow
Tachycineta thalassina

SUMMER

Size: 5¼" (13.5 cm)

Male: Dull emerald green crown, nape, and back. Violet-blue wings and tail. White chest and belly. White cheeks with white extending above the eyes. Wings extend beyond the tail when perching.

Female: same as male, only duller

Juvenile: similar to adult of the same sex

Nest: cavity; female and male build nest in tree cavities, old woodpecker holes or nest box; 1 brood per year

Eggs: 4–6; white without markings

Incubation: 13–14 days; female incubates

Fledging: 18–24 days; female and male feed the young

Migration: complete, to Central and South America

Food: insects

Compare: Similar size as the Cliff Swallow (p. 107) which has a distinctive tan-to-rust pattern on the head. Barn Swallow (p. 77) has a distinctive, deeply forked tail. The Tree Swallow (p. 75) is mostly deep blue, lacking any emerald green of the Violet-green Swallow.

Stan's Notes: A solitary nester in tree cavities and rarely beneath cliff overhangs. Like Tree Swallows, it can be attracted with a nest box. Will search for miles for errant feathers to line its nest. Tail is short and wing tips extend beyond the end of it, seen when perching. Returns to Nevada in late April and begins nesting in May. Young often leave the nest by June. On cloudy days they look black but on sunny days they look metallic green.

Green-tailed Towhee

Pipilo chlorurus

Size: 7¼" (18.5 cm)

Male: A unique yellowish-green back, wings, and tail. Dark-gray chest and face. Bright-white throat with black stripes. Rusty-red crown.

Female: same as male

Juvenile: olive-green with heavy streaking on breast and belly, lacks crown and throat markings of adult

Nest: cup; female constructs; 1–2 broods per year

Eggs: 3–5; white with brown markings

Incubation: 12–14 days; female and male incubate

Fledging: 10–14 days; female and male feed young

Migration: complete, to Arizona, New Mexico, Mexico, and Central America

Food: insects, seeds, fruit

Compare: Spotted Towhee (p. 27) is black with rusty sides, appearing nothing like Green-tailed Towhee. Green-tailed's unusual color, short wings, long tail, and large bill make it an easy bird to identify.

Stan's Notes: A common bird of shrubby hillsides and sagebrush mountain slopes as high as 7,000 feet (2,150 m). Arrives in Nevada in April. Begins breeding in June. Like other towhees, searches for insects and seeds, taking a little jump forward while kicking backward with both feet. Known to scurry away from trouble, jumping to ground without opening its wings and running across the ground.

Lewis's Woodpecker

Melanerpes lewis

YEAR-ROUND WINTER

Size: 10¾" (27.5 cm)

Male: Dull-green head and back. Distinctive gray collar and breast. Deep-red face and a light-red belly.

Female: same as male

Juvenile: similar to adult, with a brown head, lacking the red face

Nest: cavity; male and female excavate; 1 brood per year

Eggs: 4–8; white without markings

Incubation: 13–14 days; female and male incubate

Fledging: 28–34 days; female and male feed young

Migration: non-migrator to partial migrator; will move around to find food in winter

Food: insects, nuts, seeds, berries

Compare: Male Williamson's Sapsucker (p. 51) has a black back and large white wing patches, unlike the Lewis's dull green back and lack of wing patches.

Stan's Notes: Large and handsome woodpecker of western states. First collected and named in 1805 by Lewis and Clark in Montana. During breeding season, it feeds exclusively on adult insects rather than grubs, like other woodpeckers. Prefers open pine forests and areas with recent forest fires. Excavates in dead or soft wood. Uses same cavity year after year. Tends to mate for long term. Doesn't migrate, but moves around in winter to search for food such as pine nuts (seeds).

female
p. 189

male

Mallard

Anas platyrhynchos

YEAR-ROUND

Size: 19–21" (48–53 cm)

Male: Large, bulbous green head, white necklace, and rust-brown or chestnut chest. Gray-and-white sides. Yellow bill. Orange legs and feet.

Female: brown with an orange-and-black bill and blue-and-white wing mark (speculum)

Juvenile: same as female but with a yellow bill

Nest: ground; female builds; 1 brood per year

Eggs: 7–10; greenish to whitish, unmarked

Incubation: 26–30 days; female incubates

Fledging: 42–52 days; female leads the young to food

Migration: non-migrator to partial migrator in Nevada

Food: seeds, plants, aquatic insects; will come to ground feeders offering corn

Compare: Male Northern Shoveler (p. 299) has a white chest with rusty sides and a very large, spoon-shaped bill. Breeding male Northern Pintail (p. 191) has long tail feathers and a brown head. Look for the green head and yellow bill to identify the male Mallard.

Stan's Notes: A familiar dabbling duck of lakes and ponds. Also found in rivers, streams and some backyards. Tips forward to feed on vegetation on the bottom of shallow water. The name "Mallard" comes from the Latin word *masculus,* meaning "male," referring to the male's habit of taking no part in raising the young. Male and female have white underwings and white tails, but only the male has black central tail feathers that curl upward. Unlike the female, the male doesn't quack. Returns to its birthplace each year.

female
p. 187

male

Northern Shoveler
Spatula clypeata

YEAR-ROUND
SUMMER
WINTER

Size: 19–21" (48–53 cm)

Male: Medium-sized duck with an iridescent green head, rust sides, white chest. Extraordinarily large, spoon-shaped bill, almost always held pointed toward the water.

Female: brown and black all over, green wing patch (speculum), and a large spoon-shaped bill

Juvenile: same as female

Nest: ground; female builds; 1 brood per year

Eggs: 9–12; olive without markings

Incubation: 22–25 days; female incubates

Fledging: 30–60 days; female leads the young to food

Migration: complete, to Arizona, New Mexico, Mexico, and Central America; non-migrator in parts of Nevada

Food: aquatic insects, plants

Compare: Male Mallard (p. 297) is similar, but it lacks the large spoon-shaped bill.

Stan's Notes: One of several species of shovelers. Called "Shoveler" due to the peculiar, shovel-like shape of its bill. Given the common name "Northern" because it is the only species of these ducks in North America. Seen in shallow wetlands, ponds, and small lakes in flocks of 5–10 birds. Flocks fly in tight formation. Swims low in water, pointing its large bill toward the water as if it's too heavy to lift. Usually swims in tight circles while feeding. Feeds mainly by filtering tiny aquatic insects and plants from the surface of the water with its bill. Female gathers plant material and forms it into a nest a short distance from the water.

in flight

female
p. 315

male

Common Merganser

Mergus merganser

YEAR-ROUND
WINTER

Size: 26–28" (66–71 cm)

Male: Long, thin, duck-like bird with a green head and black back. White sides, chest, and neck. Long, pointed orange bill. Often looks black-and-white in poor light.

Female: same size and shape as the male, with a rust-red head and ragged "hair," gray body, white chest and chin

Juvenile: same as female

Nest: cavity; female lines an old woodpecker hole, a natural cavity, or nest box; 1 brood per year

Eggs: 9–11; ivory without markings

Incubation: 28–33 days; female incubates

Fledging: 60–70 days; female feeds the young

Migration: non-migrator to partial; moves into Nevada for the winter

Food: small fish, aquatic insects, amphibians

Compare: Male Mallard (p. 297) is smaller and lacks the black back and long, pointed orange bill.

Stan's Notes: Seen on any open water during the winter but more common along large rivers than lakes. A large, shallow-water diver that feeds on fish in 10–15 feet (3–4.5 m) of water. Bill has a fine, serrated-like edge that helps catch slippery fish. Female often lays some eggs in other merganser nests (egg dumping), resulting in up to 15 young in some broods. Male leaves the female once she starts incubating. Orphans are accepted by other merganser mothers with young. Fast flight, often low and close to the water, in groups but not in formation. Usually not vocal except for an alarm call.

301

female
p. 337

male

Bullock's Oriole
Icterus bullockii

SUMMER

Size: 8" (20 cm)

Male: Bright-orange-and-black bird. Black crown, eye line, nape, chin, back, and wings with a bold white patch on wings.

Female: dull-yellow overall, pale-white belly, white wing bars on gray-to-black wings

Juvenile: similar to female

Nest: pendulous; female and male build; 1 brood per year

Eggs: 4–6; pale white to gray, brown markings

Incubation: 12–14 days; female incubates

Fledging: 12–14 days; female and male feed young

Migration: complete, to Mexico and Central America

Food: insects, berries, nectar; visits nectar feeders

Compare: Look for Bullock's bright markings and thin black line running through each eye.

Stan's Notes: So closely related to Baltimore Orioles of the eastern US, at one time both were considered a single species. Interbreeds with Baltimores where their ranges overlap. Most common in Nevada, where cottonwood trees grow along rivers and other wetlands. Also found at edges of clearings, in city parks, on farms and along irrigation ditches. Hanging sock-like nest is constructed of plant fibers such as inner bark of junipers and willows. When building a nest, it will incorporate hair, grasses, and other soft materials as it builds.

female
p. 135

male

Black-headed Grosbeak
Pheucticus melanocephalus

Size: 8" (20 cm)

Male: Stocky bird with burnt-orange chest, neck, and rump. Black head, tail, and wings. Irregularly shaped white wing patches. Large bill, with upper bill darker than lower.

Female: appears like an overgrown sparrow, overall brown with a lighter breast and belly, large two-toned bill, prominent white eyebrows, yellow wing linings, as seen in flight

Juvenile: similar to adult of the same sex

Nest: cup; female builds; 1 brood per year

Eggs: 3–4; pale green or bluish, brown markings

Incubation: 11–13 days; female and male incubate

Fledging: 11–13 days; female and male feed young

Migration: complete, to Mexico, Central America, and South America

Food: seeds, insects, fruit; comes to seed feeders

Compare: Same size as the male Evening Grosbeak (p. 339), but male Black-headed has an orange breast and lacks a yellow belly. Male Bullock's Oriole (p. 301) has more white on the wings than the male Black-headed. Look for Black-headed's large bicolored bill.

Stan's Notes: A cosmopolitan bird that nests in a wide variety of habitats, seeming to prefer the foothills slightly more than other places. Both the male and female sing and will aggressively defend the nest against intruders. Song is very similar to American Robin's (p. 251) and Western Tanager's (p. 335), making it hard to tell them apart by song. Males don't get adult plumage until 2 years of age. Comes to seed feeders.

male

female
p. 97

yellow
male

House Finch

Haemorhous mexicanus

YEAR-ROUND

Size: 5" (13 cm)

Male: Small finch with a red-to-orange face, throat, chest, and rump. Brown cap. Brown marking behind eyes. White belly with brown streaks. Brown wings with white streaks.

Female: brown with a heavily streaked white chest

Juvenile: similar to female

Nest: cup, sometimes in cavities; female builds; several broods per year

Eggs: 4–5; pale blue, lightly marked

Incubation: 12–14 days; female incubates

Fledging: 15–19 days; female and male feed the young

Migration: non-migrator to partial migrator; moves around to find food

Food: seeds, fruit, leaf buds; visits seed feeders and feeders that offer grape jelly

Compare: Male Cassin's Finch (p. 119) is similar, but it is rosy red, unlike the orange-red of male House Finch, and it lacks a brown cap. Look for the streaked chest and belly and the brown cap to help identify the male House Finch.

Stan's Notes: Can be common at feeders. A social bird, visits feeders in small flocks. Likes to nest in hanging flower baskets. Male sings a loud, cheerful warbling song. Historically it occurred from the Pacific to the Rockies, with only a few reaching the eastern side. Now found across the US. Suffers from a disease that causes the eyes to crust, resulting in blindness and death. Rarely, some males are yellow (see inset) instead of red, probably due to poor diet.

female
p. 119

male

Cassin's Finch
Haemorhous cassinii

YEAR-ROUND
WINTER

Size: 6½" (16 cm)

Male: Overall light wash of crimson red with an especially bright-red crown. Distinct brown streaks on back and wings. White belly.

Female: overall brown to gray, fine black streaks on the back and wings, heavily streaked white chest and belly

Juvenile: similar to female

Nest: cup; female builds; 1–2 broods per year

Eggs: 3–5; bluish green with brown markings

Incubation: 12–14 days; female incubates

Fledging: 14–18 days; female and male feed young

Migration: partial migrator to non-migrator; will move around to find food

Food: seeds, insects, fruits, berries; will visit seed feeders

Compare: Male House Finch (p. 307) has a brown cap, is heavily streaked on its flanks, and is orange-red. Much more red than the Gray-crowned Rosy-Finch (p. 117).

Stan's Notes: This is a mountain finch of coniferous forests. Usually forages for seeds on the ground, but eats evergreen buds and aspen and willow catkins. A colony nester, depending on the regional source of food. The more food available, the larger the colony. Male sings a rapid warble, often imitating other birds, such as jays, tanagers, and grosbeaks. A cowbird host.

female
p. 333

male

Red Crossbill
Loxia curvirostra

YEAR-ROUND WINTER

Size: 6½" (16 cm)

Male: Sparrow-sized bird, dirty-red to orange with bright-red crown and rump. Long, pointed, crossed bill. Dark-brown wings and a short dark-brown tail.

Female: pale-yellow chest, light-gray throat patch, a crossed bill, dark-brown wings and tail

Juvenile: streaked brownish with tinges of yellow, bill gradually crosses about 2 weeks after fledging

Nest: cup; female builds; 1 brood per year

Eggs: 3–4; bluish white with brown markings

Incubation: 14–18 days; female incubates

Fledging: 16–20 days; female and male feed young

Migration: non-migrator to irruptive; moves around the state in winter to find food

Food: seeds, leaf buds; comes to seed feeders

Compare: Larger than the male House Finch (p. 307) and has a unique crossed bill.

Stan's Notes: The long crossed bill is adapted for extracting seeds from pine and spruce cones, its favorite food. Often dangles upside down like a parrot to reach cones. Also seen on the ground where it eats grit, which helps digest food. Nests in low elevation coniferous forests. Plumage can be highly variable among individuals. While it is a resident nester, migrating crossbills from farther north move into Nevada during winter, searching for food, increasing populations during some winters. This irruptive behavior makes it more common in some winters and nonexistent in others.

female p. 183

male

Redhead
Aythya americana

SUMMER
WINTER

Size: 19" (48 cm)

Male: Rich-red head and neck with a black breast and tail, gray sides, and smoky-gray wings and back. Tricolored bill with a light-blue base, white ring, and black tip.

Female: soft-brown, plain-looking duck with gray-to-white wing linings, a rounded top of head, and a gray bill with a black tip

Juvenile: similar to female

Nest: cup; female builds; 1 brood per year

Eggs: 9–14; white without markings

Incubation: 24–28 days; female incubates

Fledging: 56–73 days; female shows young what to eat

Migration: complete migrator, to southwestern states, Mexico, and Central America

Food: seeds, aquatic plants, insects

Compare: The male Northern Shoveler (p. 299) has a green head and rusty sides, unlike the red head and gray sides of the male Redhead.

Stan's Notes: A duck of permanent large bodies of water. Forages along the shoreline, feeding on seeds, aquatic plants, and insects. Usually builds nest directly on the water's surface, using large mats of vegetation. Female lays up to 75 percent of its eggs in the nests of other Redheads and several other duck species. Nests primarily in the Prairie Pothole region of the northern Great Plains. The overall populations seem to be increasing at about 2–3 percent each year.

male
p. 301

in flight

female

Common Merganser

Mergus merganser

YEAR-ROUND
WINTER

Size: 26–28" (66–71 cm)

Female: Long, thin, duck-like bird with a rust-red head and ragged "hair." Gray body and white chest and chin. Long, pointed orange bill.

Male: same size and shape as the female, but with a green head, a black back and white sides

Juvenile: same as female

Nest: cavity; female lines an old woodpecker hole, a natural cavity, or nest box; 1 brood per year

Eggs: 9–11; ivory without markings

Incubation: 28–33 days; female incubates

Fledging: 70–80 days; female feeds the young

Migration: non-migrator to partial; moves into Nevada for the winter

Food: small fish, aquatic insects

Compare: Hard to confuse with other birds. Look for a rust-red head with ragged "hair," a white chin and a long, pointed orange bill to identify.

Stan's Notes: Seen on any open water during the winter but more common along large rivers than lakes. A large, shallow-water diver that feeds on fish in 10–15 feet (3–4.5 m) of water. Bill has a fine, serrated-like edge that helps catch slippery fish. The female often lays some eggs in other merganser nests (egg dumping), resulting in up to 15 young in some broods. Male leaves the female once she starts incubating. Orphans are accepted by other merganser mothers with young. Fast flight, often low and close to the water, in groups but not in formation. Usually not vocal except for an alarm call that sounds like a muffled quack.

in flight

SUMMER
MIGRATION

Snowy Egret
Egretta thula

Size: 22–26" (56–66 cm); up to 3½' wingspan

Male: All-white bird with black bill. Black legs. Bright-yellow feet. Long feather plumes on head, neck, and back during breeding season.

Female: same as male

Juvenile: similar to adult, but backs of legs are yellow

Nest: platform; female and male build; 1 brood per year

Eggs: 3–5; light blue-green without markings

Incubation: 20–24 days; female and male incubate

Fledging: 28–30 days; female and male feed the young

Migration: complete, to southern Arizona and Mexico

Food: aquatic insects, small fish

Compare: This is the only all-white egret in the state. Look for the black bill and yellow feet of Snowy Egret to help identify.

Stan's Notes: Common in wetlands. Colonies may include up to several hundred nests. Nests are low in shrubs 5–10 feet (1.5–3 m) tall or constructs a nest on the ground, usually mixed among other egret and heron nests. Chicks hatch days apart (asynchronous), leading to starvation of last to hatch. Will actively "hunt" prey by moving around quickly, stirring up small fish and aquatic insects with its feet. In the breeding state, a yellow patch at the base of bill and the yellow feet turn orange-red. Was hunted to near extinction in the late 1800s for its feathers.

in flight

breeding

juvenile

winter

Herring Gull
Larus argentatus

MIGRATION WINTER

Size: 23–26" (58–66 cm); up to 5' wingspan

Male: White with slate-gray wings. Black wing tips with tiny white spots. Yellow bill with an orange-red spot near the tip of the lower bill (mandible). Pinkish legs and feet. Winter plumage has gray speckles on head and neck.

Female: same as male

Juvenile: mottled brown to gray, with a black bill

Nest: ground; female and male construct; 1 brood per year

Eggs: 2–3; olive with brown markings

Incubation: 24–28 days; female and male incubate

Fledging: 35–50 days; female and male feed the young

Migration: complete, to West Coast from British Columbia to Mexico

Food: fish, insects, clams, eggs, baby birds

Compare: Look for the orange-red spot on the bill to help identify the Herring Gull.

Stan's Notes: A common gull of large lakes. An opportunistic bird, scavenging for human food in dumpsters, parking lots, and other places with garbage. Takes eggs and young from other bird nests. Often drops clams and other shellfish from heights to break the shells and get to the soft interior. Nests in colonies, returning to the same site annually. Lines its nest with grass and seaweed. It takes about four years for the juveniles to obtain adult plumage. Adults have spotted heads during winter.

breeding

in flight

chick-feeding
adult

American White Pelican
Pelecanus erythrorhynchos

Size: 60–64" (152–163 cm); up to 9' wingspan

Male: Large white pelican with an enormous bright-yellow-to-orange bill. Yellow legs and feet. Black wing tips and trailing edge of wings. Breeding plumage has a bright-orange bill, legs and feet. Chick-feeding adult (an adult that is feeding young) has a gray-black crown.

Female: same as male

Juvenile: duller white than adult, with a brownish head and neck

Nest: ground, scraped-out depression rimmed with dirt; female and male build; 1 brood per year

Eggs: 1–3; white without markings

Incubation: 29–36 days; male and female incubate

Fledging: 60–70 days; female and male feed the young

Migration: complete, to California, Arizona, and Mexico

Food: fish

Compare: Large and obvious bird with huge bill.

Stan's Notes: Often seen in large groups on the larger lakes and reservoirs of Nevada. Doesn't dive to catch fish, like coastal Brown Pelicans. Instead, groups swim and dip their bills simultaneously into water to scoop up fish. Groups fly in a large V, often gliding, followed by simultaneous flapping. Large flocks swirl on columns of rising warm air (thermals) on hot days. Breeding adults typically grow a flat, fibrous plate on the upper bill, which drops off after the eggs hatch. Usually silent; gives short grunts at the nesting colony.

male

female

Lesser Goldfinch
Spinus psaltria

YEAR-ROUND
SUMMER

Size: 4½" (11 cm)

Male: Striking bright yellow beneath from chin to base of tail. Black head, tail and wings. White patches on wings. Eastern variety has a black back. Western has a green back.

Female: dull yellow underneath, lacks a black head and back

Juvenile: same as female

Nest: cup; female builds; 1–2 broods per year

Eggs: 4–5; pale blue without markings

Incubation: 10–12 days; female incubates

Fledging: 12–14 days; female and male feed young

Migration: partial to non-migrator; will move around the state to find food

Food: seeds, insects; will come to seed feeders

Compare: The male American Goldfinch (p. 325) is slightly larger and has a yellow back, unlike the greenish back of male eastern Lesser Goldfinch or the black back of male western Lesser Goldfinch.

Stan's Notes: The western males have greenish backs, while males in the eastern range (Texas) have entirely black heads and backs. Some females are extremely pale. Prefers forest edges with a consistent water source. Unlike many other birds, its diet is about 96 percent seed, even during peak insect season. Will come to seed feeders. Late summer nesters. Male feeds the incubating female by regurgitating seeds. Pairs stay together all winter. Winter flocks can number in the hundreds.

male

winter male

female

American Goldfinch
Spinus tristis

YEAR-ROUND
WINTER

Size: 5" (13 cm)

Male: Canary-yellow finch with a black forehead and tail. Black wings with white wing bars. White rump. No markings on the chest. Winter male is similar to the female.

Female: dull olive-yellow plumage with brown wings; lacks a black forehead

Juvenile: same as female

Nest: cup; female builds; 1 brood per year

Eggs: 4–6; pale blue without markings

Incubation: 12–14 days; female incubates

Fledging: 11–17 days; female and male feed the young

Migration: partial migrator to non-migrator; small flocks of up to 20 birds move around to find food

Food: seeds, insects; will come to seed feeders

Compare: The Pine Siskin (p. 95) and female House Finch (p. 97) both have a streaked chest. Male Yellow Warbler (p. 331) is all yellow with orange streaks on chest.

Stan's Notes: A common backyard resident. Most often found in open fields, scrubby areas, and woodlands. Enjoys Nyjer seed in feeders. Lines its nest with the silky down from wild thistle. Almost always in small flocks. Twitters while it flies. Flight is roller coaster-like. Often called Wild Canary due to the male's canary-colored plumage. Male sings a pleasant, high-pitched song. Moves only far enough south to find food.

SUMMER
MIGRATION

Common Yellowthroat
Geothlypis trichas

Size: 5" (13 cm)

Male: Olive-brown with a bright-yellow throat and chest, a white belly, and a distinctive black mask outlined in white. Long, thin, pointed black bill.

Female: similar to male but lacks a black mask

Juvenile: same as female

Nest: cup; female builds; 2 broods per year

Eggs: 3–5; white with brown markings

Incubation: 11–12 days; female incubates

Fledging: 10–11 days; female and male feed the young

Migration: complete migrator, to Arizona, Mexico, and Central America

Food: insects

Compare: The male American Goldfinch (p. 325) has a black forehead and wings. Male Yellow Warbler (p. 331) has fine orange streaks on chest and lacks the black mask. The Yellow-rumped Warbler (p. 235) only has patches of yellow and lacks the yellow chest of the Yellowthroat.

Stan's Notes: A common warbler of open fields and marshes. Sings a cheerful, well-known "witchity-witchity-witchity-witchity" song from deep within tall grasses. Male sings from prominent perches and while he hunts. He performs a curious courtship display, bouncing in and out of tall grass while singing a mating song. Female builds a nest low to the ground. Young remain dependent on their parents longer than most other warblers. A frequent cowbird host.

Orange-crowned Warbler
Oreothlypis celata

Size: 5" (13 cm)

Male: An overall pale-yellow bird with a dark line through eyes. Faint streaking on sides and chest. Tawny-orange crown, often invisible. Small thin bill.

Female: same as male, but very slightly duller, often indistinguishable in the field

Juvenile: same as adults

Nest: cup; female builds; 1 brood per year

Eggs: 3–6; white with brown markings

Incubation: 12–14 days; female incubates

Fledging: 8–10 days; female and male feed young

Migration: complete migrator, to Arizona, California, Mexico, and Central America

Food: insects, fruit, nectar

Compare: Yellow Warbler (p. 331) is brighter yellow with orange streaking on the male's chest. Male Common Yellowthroat (p. 327) has a distinctive black mask.

Stan's Notes: A widespread warbler and nesting resident in Nevada, but is often seen more during migration when large groups move together. Builds a bulky, well-concealed nest on the ground with nest rim at ground level. Known to drink flower nectar. The orange crown tends to be hidden and is rarely seen in the field. A widespread breeder, from western Texas to Alaska and across Canada.

male

female

Yellow Warbler
Setophaga petechia

Size: 5" (13 cm)

Male: Yellow with thin orange streaks on the chest and belly. Long, pointed dark bill.

Female: same as male but lacks orange streaks

Juvenile: similar to female but much duller

Nest: cup; female builds; 1 brood per year

Eggs: 4–5; greenish white with brown markings

Incubation: 11–12 days; female incubates

Fledging: 10–12 days; female and male feed the young

Migration: complete, to Mexico, Central America, and South America

Food: insects

Compare: Orange-crowned Warbler (p. 329) is paler yellow. The male American Goldfinch (p. 325) has a black forehead and black wings. Look for the orange streaks on the chest to identify the male Yellow Warbler. The female American Goldfinch (p. 325) has white wing bars.

Stan's Notes: Most widespread and second most common warbler in the state, seen in gardens and shrubby areas near water. A prolific insect eater, gleaning caterpillars and other insects from tree leaves. Male sings a string of notes that sound like "sweet, sweet, sweet, I'm-so-sweet!" Begins to migrate south in August. Returns in late April. Males arrive in spring before females to claim territories. Migrates at night in mixed flocks of warblers. Rests and feeds during the day.

male
p. 311

female

Red Crossbill
Loxia curvirostra

Size: 6½" (16 cm)

Female: A pale yellow-gray sparrow-sized bird with a pale-yellow chest and light-gray patch on the throat. Long, pointed, crossed bill. Dark-brown wings and a short dark-brown tail.

Male: dirty-red to orange with a bright-red crown and rump, a crossed bill, dark-brown wings and a short dark-brown tail

Juvenile: streaked brownish with tinges of yellow, bill gradually crosses about 2 weeks after fledging

Nest: cup; female builds; 1 brood per year

Eggs: 3–4; bluish white with brown markings

Incubation: 14–18 days; female incubates

Fledging: 16–20 days; female and male feed young

Migration: non-migrator to irruptive; moves around in winter in search of food

Food: seeds, leaf buds; comes to seed feeders

Compare: Larger than the female American Goldfinch (p. 325). Look for the unique crossed bill to help identify.

Stan's Notes: The long crossed bill is adapted for extracting seeds from pine and spruce cones, its favorite food. Often dangles upside down like a parrot to reach cones. Also seen on the ground where it eats grit, which helps digest food. Nests in low elevation coniferous forests. Plumage can be highly variable among individuals. While it is a resident nester, migrating crossbills from farther north move into Nevada during winter, searching for food, swelling populations. This irruptive behavior makes it more common in some winters and nonexistent in others.

male

non-breeding male

female

Western Tanager
Piranga ludoviciana

Size: 7¼" (18.5 cm)

Male: A canary-yellow bird with a red head. Black back, tail, wings. One white and one yellow wing bar. Non-breeding lacks the red head.

Female: duller than male, lacking the red head

Juvenile: similar to female

Nest: cup; female builds; 1 brood per year

Eggs: 3–5; light blue with brown markings

Incubation: 14–18 days; female incubates

Fledging: 16–20 days; female and male feed young

Migration: complete, to Mexico and Central America

Food: insects, fruit

Compare: The unique coloring makes the breeding male Tanager easy to identify. Male American Goldfinch (p. 325) male has a black forehead. Female Bullock's Oriole (p. 337) lacks the female Tanager's single yellow wing bars.

Stan's Notes: The male is stunning in its breeding plumage. Feeds mainly on insects, such as bees, wasps, cicadas, and grasshoppers, and to a lesser degree on fruit. The male feeds the female while she incubates. Female builds a cup nest in a horizontal fork of a coniferous tree, well away from the main trunk, 20–40 feet (6–12 m) aboveground. This is the farthest-nesting tanager species, reaching far up into the Northwest Territories of Canada. An early fall migrant, often seen migrating in late July (when non-breeding males lack red heads). Seen in many habitats during migration.

male
p. 303

female

Bullock's Oriole
Icterus bullockii

SUMMER

Size: 8" (20 cm)

Female: Dull-yellow head and chest. Gray-to-black wings with white wing bars. A pale-white belly. Gray back, as seen in flight.

Male: bright-orange-and-black bird with a bold white patch on wings

Juvenile: similar to female

Nest: pendulous; female and male build; 1 brood per year

Eggs: 4–6; pale white to gray, brown markings

Incubation: 12–14 days; female incubates

Fledging: 12–14 days; female and male feed young

Migration: complete, to Mexico and Central America

Food: insects, berries, nectar; visits nectar feeders

Compare: Smaller female Western Tanager (p. 335) has a black back, compared with the female Bullock's gray back.

Stan's Notes: So closely related to Baltimore Orioles of the eastern US, at one time both were considered a single species. Interbreeds with Baltimores where their ranges overlap. Most common in Nevada, where cottonwood trees grow alongside rivers and other wetlands. Also found at edges of clearings, in city parks, on farms and along irrigation ditches. Hanging sock-like nest is constructed of plant fibers such as inner bark of junipers and willows. Will incorporate yarn and thread into its nest if offered at the time of nest building.

male

juvenile

female

Evening Grosbeak
Coccothraustes vespertinus

YEAR-ROUND
WINTER

Size: 8" (20 cm)

Male: Striking bird with bright-yellow eyebrows, rump, and belly. Black-and-white wings and tail. Dark, dirty-yellow head and large, thick ivory-to-greenish bill.

Female: similar to male, with softer colors and a gray head and throat

Juvenile: similar to female, with a brown bill

Nest: cup; female builds; 1–2 broods per year

Eggs: 3–4; blue with brown markings

Incubation: 12–14 days; female incubates

Fledging: 13–14 days; female and male feed young

Migration: irruptive; moves around the state to find food

Food: seeds, insects, fruit; comes to seed feeders

Compare: The American Goldfinch (p. 325) is closely related, but it is much smaller. Look for the yellow eyebrows and thick bill to identify the Evening Grosbeak.

Stan's Notes: One of the largest finches. Characteristic finch-like undulating flight. Uses its unusually large bill to crack seeds, its main food source. Often seen on gravel roads eating gravel, which provides minerals, salt, and grit to grind the seeds it eats. A year-round resident in western parts of Nevada, it is more obvious during the winter because it moves in large flocks, searching for food, often coming to feeders. Sheds the outer layer of its bill during spring, exposing a blue-green bill.

SUMMER

Scott's Oriole
Icterus parisorum

Size: 9" (22.5 cm)

Male: Black head, neck, back, upper breast, and tail. Lemon-yellow belly, shoulders, and rump. Long, pointed, slightly down-curved black bill. Dark eyes. Two white wing bars.

Female: similar to male, but has much less black

Juvenile: grayer than female, yellow under belly only

Nest: pendulous; female builds; 1–2 broods a year

Eggs: 2–4; pale blue with brown markings

Incubation: 14–16 days; female incubates

Fledging: 14–16 days; female and male feed young

Migration: complete, to Mexico

Food: insects, fruit, nectar; will come to orange or grapefruit halves and nectar feeders

Compare: The female Bullock's Oriole (p. 307) has a pale-white belly. Male American Goldfinch (p. 325) is much smaller and has black on the forehead, not on the entire head.

Stan's Notes: Found in open dry areas often associated with yucca and palm. Like other oriole species, female constructs a sock-like pouch that hangs from the end of a thin branch or is woven into a hole in a palm leaf. Populations have increased over the past 100 years due to planting of palm trees. Male is yellow, not orange, like other male orioles. Hunts by gleaning insects and caterpillars from leaves. Uses its long pointed bill to poke holes in bases of flowers to get nectar. Parents feed their young by regurgitating a mixture of insects and fruit. Named after General Winfield Scott, who fought in the Mexican War.

Western Kingbird
Tyrannus verticalis

SUMMER

Size: 9" (22.5 cm)

Male: Bright-yellow belly and yellow under wings. Gray head and chest, often with white chin. Wings and tail are dark gray to nearly black with white outer edges on tail.

Female: same as male

Juvenile: similar to adult, less yellow and more gray

Nest: cup; female and male construct; 1 brood per year

Eggs: 3–4; white with brown markings

Incubation: 18–20 days; female incubates

Fledging: 16–18 days; female and male feed young

Migration: complete, to Mexico and Central America

Food: insects, berries

Compare: Western Meadowlark (p. 345) shares the yellow belly of Western Kingbird, but it has a distinctive black V-shaped necklace.

Stan's Notes: A bird of open country, frequently seen sitting on top of the same shrub or fence post. Hunts by watching for crickets, bees, grasshoppers, and other insects and flying out to catch them, then returns to perch. Parents teach young how to hunt, bringing wounded insects back to the nest for the young to chase. Returns in April. Builds nest in May, often in a fork of a small single-trunk tree. Common throughout Nevada, nesting in trees around homesteads and farms.

Western Meadowlark

Sturnella neglecta

YEAR-ROUND

Size: 9" (22.5 cm)

Male: Heavy-bodied bird with a short tail. Yellow chest and brown back. Prominent V-shaped black necklace. White outer tail feathers.

Female: same as male

Juvenile: same as adult

Nest: dome-shaped cup, on the ground in dense cover; female builds; 2 broods per year

Eggs: 3–5; white with brown markings

Incubation: 13–15 days; female incubates

Fledging: 11–13 days; female and male feed young

Migration: non-migrator to partial migrator

Food: insects, seeds

Compare: Western Kingbird (p. 343) shares the yellow belly, but it lacks the V-shaped black necklace. Horned Lark (p. 127) lacks the yellow chest and belly. Look for a black V marking on the chest to help identify the Meadowlark.

Stan's Notes: Most common in open country of Nevada. Named "Meadowlark" because it's a bird of meadows and sings like the larks of Europe. Not in the lark family; a blackbird family member and is related to grackles and orioles. Best known for its wonderful song—a flute-like, clear whistle. Often seen perching on fence posts but quickly dives into tall grass when approached. Like other members of the blackbird family, the meadowlark catches prey by poking its long thin bill in places such as holes in the ground or tufts of grass, where insects are hiding. Conspicuous white marks on sides of tail, seen when flying away. Overall population is down greatly due to agricultural activities and ditch mowing.

BIRDING ON THE INTERNET

Birding online is a great way to discover additional information and learn more about birds. These websites will assist you in your pursuit of birds. Web addresses sometimes change a bit, so if one no longer works, just enter the name of the group into a search engine to track down the new address.

Site	Address
Author Stan Tekiela's homepage	naturesmart.com
American Birding Association	aba.org
Lahontan Audobon Society	nevadaaudubon.org
The Cornell Lab of Ornithology	birds.cornell.edu
eBird	ebird.org
Red Rock Audubon	redrockaudubon.com

CHECKLIST/INDEX BY SPECIES

Use the boxes to check the birds you've seen.

MORE FOR NEVADA BY STAN TEKIELA

Identification Guides
- Birds of Prey of the West Field Guide
- Birds of the Southwest
- Stan Tekiela's Birding for Beginners: Southwest

Children's Books:
Adventure Board Book Series
- Floppers & Loppers
- Paws & Claws
- Peepers & Peekers
- Snouts & Sniffers

Children's Books
- C is for Cardinal
- Can You Count the Critters?
- Critter Litter

Children's Books:
Wildlife Picture Books
- Baby Bear Discovers the World
- The Cutest Critter
- Do Beavers Need Blankets?
- Hidden Critters
- Some Babies Are Wild
- Super Animal Powers
- What Eats That?
- Whose Baby Butt?
- Whose Butt?
- Whose House Is That?
- Whose Track Is That?

Nature Books
- Bird Trivia
- Start Mushrooming
- A Year in Nature with Stan Tekiela

Backyard Bird Feeding Guides
- Attracting & Feeding Bluebirds
- Attracting & Feeding Cardinals
- Attracting & Feeding Finches
- Attracting & Feeding Hummingbirds
- Attracting & Feeding Orioles
- Attracting & Feeding Woodpeckers

Favorite Wildlife Series
- Bald Eagles
- Bears of North America
- Hummingbirds
- Loons
- Owls
- Wolves, Coyotes & Foxes

Our Love of Wildlife Series
- Our Love of Loons
- Our Love of Owls

Wildlife Appreciation Series
- Backyard Birds
- Bird Migration
- Cranes, Herons & Egrets
- Deer, Elk & Moose
- Wild Birds

Nature Appreciation Series
- Bird Nests
- Feathers
- Wildflowers

Nature's Wild Cards (playing cards)
- Bears
- Birds of the Southwest
- Hummingbirds
- Loons
- Mammals of the Southwest
- Owls
- Raptors
- Trees of the Southwest

ABOUT THE AUTHOR

Naturalist, wildlife photographer, and writer Stan Tekiela is the originator of the popular state-specific field guide series that includes the *Birds of California Field Guide*. Stan has authored more than 190 educational books, including field guides, quick guides, nature books, children's books, and more, presenting many species of animals and plants.

With a Bachelor of Science degree in natural history from the University of Minnesota and as an active professional naturalist for more than 30 years, Stan studies and photographs wildlife throughout the United States and Canada. He has received national and regional awards for his books and photographs and is also a well-known columnist and radio personality. His syndicated column appears in more than 25 newspapers, and his wildlife programs are broadcast on a number of Midwest radio stations. You can follow Stan on Facebook and Twitter or contact him via his website, naturesmart.com.